SACRAMENTO

"Sacramento's•Enterprises"
by•Douglas•K.•Curley

Windsor•Publications,•Inc.
Chatsworth,•California

THE HEART OF CALIFORNIA

SACRAMENTO

A · CONTEMPORARY · PORTRAIT · BY · RICHARD · TRAINOR

Windsor Publications, Inc.—Book Division
Managing Editor: Karen Story
Design Director: Alexander D'Anca
Photo Director: Susan L. Wells
Executive Editor: Pamela Schroeder

Staff for *Sacramento: Heart of California*
Senior Manuscript Editor: Jerry Mosher
Photo Editor: Lisa Willinger
Editor, Corporate Profiles: Jeffrey Reeves
Production Editor, Corporate Profiles: Justin Scupine
Proofreader: Annette Nibblett Arrieta
Customer Service Manager: Phyllis Feldman-Schroeder
Editorial Assistants: Elizabeth Anderson, Lori Erbaugh, Kim
    Kievman, Michael Nugwynne, Kathy B. Peyser, Theresa J. Solis
Publisher's Representatives, Corporate Profiles: Beverly Cornell,
    Harriett Holmes
Layout Artist, Corporate Profiles: Bonnie Felt
Layout Artist, Editorial: Michael Burg
Designer: Thomas McTighe

Library of Congress Cataloging-in-Publication Data
Trainor, Richard, 1951-
Sacramento : the heart of California : a contemporary portrait /
    by Richard Trainor.
p. 192 cm. 23 x 31
Includes bibliographical references and index.
ISBN 0-89781-388-X
1. Sacramento (Calif.)—Description. I. Title.
F869.S12T73 1991   90-25732
979.4′54—dc20   CIP

Windsor Publications, Inc.
Elliot Martin, Chairman of the Board
James L. Fish III, Chief Operating Officer
Mac Buhler, Vice President/Acquisitions

*Frontispiece: The Hyatt Hotel's 15th-floor terraces afford
a spectacular view of the city. Photo by Richard Kaylin*

*Right: Festive face paint, costumes, and umbrellas adorn
participants in the annual Memorial Day weekend Dixieland Jubilee. Photo by Tom Myers*

Contents

A Capital Place

The recently recoppered dome of the State Capitol building glitters against a bright blue sky. Photo by Bob Rowan/Progressive Image Photography

A Working History: Reinventing New Helvetia

New Helvetia, Winter 1848

N Outside, the old Alcalde could hear the sodden limbs of the oaks and sycamores creaking in the wind, and farther out on the slough the ducks clacked delightedly as the first hard storm of the season loosed itself on New Helvetia in the winter of 1848.

In the crude but well-appointed three-room adobe within the three-foot-thick walls of his fort, the old Alcalde unwound the sash from his considerable belly, poured himself the nightly dram of the wild-grape brandy he'd lately begun distilling, and sat down at his desk to enter some notations in his ledgers.

Sipping, he reflected. The summer had been prosperous and the fall and winter so far gentle—nothing like the year before when the rains came early in October and caught those poor devils up on the lake and summit that would forever after bear their name. This would be an untroubled year, he hoped. This year there would be no disasters like the Donner Party to suck the resources of his settlement dry and give it an unsavory reputation. Soon the land would be part of the Union, and political intriguers like that blustering opportunist John Charles Frémont and his revolting Bear Flag gang would maybe quit this country and cease disturbing the old Alcalde and his private fiefdom of 50,000 acres.

The Mexicans who granted him this land called him Don Juan. Back home in Switzerland, they'd have called him Seigneur or Baron or Padrone. He was, as he called himself, Captain Johann Augustus Sutter, Sr., an ex-bankruptee from Berne, sole owner of an inland empire the size of a Swiss canton in the heart of the Great Valley of *Alta California*.

Next year Sutter could send for the wife and children he'd left in Berne that misty May morning 14 years before, when he had journeyed by foot and cart to Le Havre, and then on across the Atlantic to seek his fortune in the New

During Sacramento's early years, commercial activity centered on Front Street, where river steamers met the transcontinental railroad. This detail of a painting by Carl Wilhelm Hahn shows Front Street commerce and the Central Pacific Passenger Station in 1874. Courtesy, The Fine Arts Museum of San Francisco, gift of M.H. de Young Endowment Fund

Land. Now that he'd found it, all he had to do was keep it.

When he first came to the Great Valley in the summer of 1839, it was with a mostly Hawaiian settler crew. In two schooners they sailed north from Monterey, then east through the Bahia de San Francisco toward the wide mouth of the rivers. Trailing one of the schooners was a four-oared pinnace that would serve as scout boat. With the pinnace they could explore the labyrinthine waterways of the Delta, a vast maze of islands traversed by rivers, creeks, and sloughs.

Along the way, Sutter fought a skirmish or two with the native Nisenan Indians and fended off a mutiny attempt by some of the more restless members of his crew, who after three months in a boat had had their fill of exploring. Considering his options, Sutter ordered the schooners about, sailed back south, and found what looked to be a good site for his intended settlement.

It was on a high bluff just east of the confluence of the two biggest rivers on the delta. The Mexicans called the smaller, east-forking river "El Rio de los Americanos" after the Anglo trappers like Jedediah Smith who discovered and explored it in the 1820s. The bigger river bearing the American and another six rivers along with it as it rolled south into San Pablo Bay they called the "Buenaventura"—The Good Fortune.

The old Alcalde's fortunes had taken a turn for the good in the eight and a half years since he first established his fort on the knoll overlooking Burns Slough. He'd befriended the Indians and put them in his employ, tilling the rich black soil. Now the valley was beginning to fill with settlers coming over the Sierras on the Emigrant Trail,

or down the valley from the Oregon Trail; hundreds of settlers, good, God-fearing Mormons and Protestants or Germanic Catholics like himself and his neighbor, A.J. Leidesdorf. Leidesdorf, like Sutter, lived on a vast Mexican land grant just up the American on the river's north bank. After those first years of backbreaking labor, staking out and building their settlements, Sutter and Leidesdorf had lately begun to enjoy more gracious living, and the land now showed the fruit of their labors.

In the long mild summers the fields gave forth with tall gold stalks of wheat and barley, the broad expanses of waving grain giving way every so often to patches of green where an occasional cornfield or fruit orchard was planted.

And the harvest of the valley's first manufactures—woolen blankets and "California banknotes" (tanned hides that were exchanged as currency)—were also adding to Sutter's wealth.

The future seemed limitless, thought the old Alcalde as he shut his books, slipped off his boots and lit a cheroot. He raised the brandy appraisingly, swirling the tawny liquid but sipping it cautiously. The brandy needed more than a little refinement: it eventually had the desired soothing effect but first you had to endure a fiery jolt that hit your belly with the dead weight of a musket ball. Maybe different grapes, he mused.

But if the vagaries of distillation turned out to be the thorniest problem he would face that winter, John Sutter would count himself a happy man. Dimming the wick of his lamp, Sutter lay down to sleep the dreamless sleep of the innocents. By the next evening, the old Alcalde's world would be totally undone.

Facing page: Acorns were a principal food of the Central California Indians. Since acorns could be stored and used when other foods were scarce, Indians could live in permanent villages with concentrated populations. The acorns were ground, leached, made into mush, and then boiled in large baskets. The oak forests that once abounded in the area provided a large supply of acorns. Courtesy, Norman L. Wilson

Left: Prospectors used sluices filled with flowing water to separate the heavy gold from the lighter surrounding dirt. Earth was shoveled into water passing through the sluice, and the gold, due to its weight, accumulated behind the riffles on the sluice's bottom. These prospectors were photographed at Spanish Flat in 1852. (Windsor file photo)

"Gold on the American!"

The following afternoon—January 28, 1848—James Marshall, Sutter's foreman and partner in the lumber mill they owned up in Coloma on the middle fork of the American River, galloped through the fort gates and demanded to see Sutter in private. Sutter dismissed the cronies and shopkeepers who usually kept him company and asked Marshall what was on his mind. The mill foreman dug in his pocket and tossed a vial filled with metal flakes on Sutter's desk.

"What's this?" asked Sutter.

"Gold," Marshall replied.

Sutter laughed.

It was one of the last moments of genuine amusement poor John Sutter would ever have.

Sutter and Marshall swore themselves to secrecy when tests proved the metal was gold. But word of the discovery somehow leaked out to Samuel Brannan, a merchant who had a store at Sutter's Fort. Brannan also owned a newspaper in Yerba Buena, the settlement by the San Francisco Bay.

One afternoon, not two months after Marshall's discovery, Brannan came barrelling down the streets of Yerba Buena waving a stack of newspapers and shouting at the top of his lungs: "Gold, gold, gold on the American River!"

The news literally shook the world. Immigrants soon flooded the Great Valley by the thousands, and from every point of the compass—Europe, South America, Asia. In short order, Yerba Buena was transformed from a sleepy Spanish town on the bay to a bustling city called San Fran-

cisco. New Helvetia was effaced and replaced by Sacramento, a city that would endure floods, fires, miasmas, and money panics. In the process, the old Alcalde's *buena ventura* ran out. Within four years of the Gold Rush, John Sutter went from baron to bankrupt.

The World Rushes to Sacramento

The Gold Rush ruined the naive and trusting Sutter, whose vast holdings were soon reduced to a stack of worthless deeds by riffraff and sharpers who squatted or swindled him out of his fortune. But it also gave birth to the city of Sacramento and placed it front and center on the world's stage as the destination for which every man of ambition was headed.

Gold was found not only on the American, but also on the other rivers feeding the Sacramento: the Yuba, the Bear, the Feather, the Cosumnes, and the Mokelumne rivers, as well as on all of their feeder streams. In the first year of the Gold Rush, miners took in 11,866 ounces of gold worth $245,000. The next year the numbers jumped to 491,072 ounces worth upward of $10 million. By the time the Gold Rush hit its peak in 1852, those numbers had soared to nearly 4 million ounces of gold worth $81 million, a figure that would equal roughly $2 billion today.

Correspondingly, the City of Sacramento was the site for one of the most explosive periods of growth a city has ever witnessed. There were maybe 500 settlers in the Sacramento Valley before Marshall's discovery. By October 1849, the population of Sacramento City, as it was called, had reached 2,000. Two months later, the population nearly doubled, doubling again the next year to 6,820. By 1855, when gold production began to dip, the city's population began leveling off at 12,000.

With an ever-expanding population mushrooming at so prodigious a rate, and assets piling up quicker than chips in a high-stakes game of faro, the settlement on the bluff became a city along the Sacramento River Embarcadero. In 1849, it was laid out as such by Captain W.H. Warner of the Army Corps of Engineers. Warner platted a city of 320-foot-square blocks bisected by alleys that ran east and west, laying it out in a rectilinear grid from B through Y, and Front through 31st streets. Assisting Warner with the sur-

veying was a young army lieutenant from West Point, living out west and trying to forget his miserable showing in the just-concluded Mexican War—William Tecumseh Sherman.

During that heady era defined by gold, one could either prospect in the fields or prospect in town off those working the fields. While many a gold miner fared profitably with rocker, pan, and Long Tom, those working the mercantile lodes of the towns usually did much better. San Francisco, the jumping off point of the Gold Rush (it literally was just that; hundreds of clipper ships lay ghostlike in the harbor, abandoned by their crews), soon rivalled New Orleans and New York in volume of daily trade. And Sacramento, the jumping off point for the mines themselves, was both their transportation hub and supply center. One miner, writing from San Francisco in the spring of 1849, told his son-in-law that "freights and transportation expenses are enormously high. From this to mines, freight is $6 per 100 lbs., and from thence to the mines, the whole charge for transportation is nearly equal to one dollar per pound. Thus a barrel of flour costing here $14 . . . would actually cost the vendor at the mines $152 per barrel!"

The Rise of the Railroads

With Sacramento as the transportation hub of overland stages heading east to the mines, and with freight and provision costs so astronomically high, it was only a matter of time before someone hit on the idea of replacing the dusty, low-capacity stages with a train running from Sacramento.

In 1854, a local businessman named Charles Lincoln Wilson began talking openly about this idea. Wilson began looking for an engineer with gumption enough to take up such a gamble, eventually heading back east to enlist the services of the man who had bridged the difficult Niagara Gorge.

Theodore Dahone Judah was then 27 years old when Wilson hired him to build the first railroad west of the Mississippi. It was an inspired stroke on Wilson's part: Judah was a visionary who saw the Sacramento Valley Rail Road as the first link in what would eventually become a transcontinental system joining both coasts of the republic.

In early 1855 ground was broken for the SVRR. A year later, two trains daily were running the 22 miles from Sacramento to Folsom, which, in turn, became the headquarters for stages serving the northern mines, dispatching 20 stages daily to mining camps like Iowa Hill, Mormon Island, and Whisky Bar. The SVRR was operating at a $100,000 annual profit when it was sold in 1865 to a new railroad company, the Central Pacific.

When Judah's railroad proved a successful enterprise, his credibility went up. Now talk of a transcontinental railroad didn't seem such a pipe dream. Four Sacramento businessmen—Collis P. Huntington and his hardware store partner Mark Hopkins, and Leland Stanford and Charles Crocker—formed the Central Pacific and hired "Crazy Judah," as derisive locals once called him, to engineer a route over the Sierras.

Using laborers mostly imported from China, the CP began construction in January 1863. The first 18-mile leg east took almost a year. But with more and more Chinese workers

Facing page, top: The Huntington and Hopkins hardware store at 54 K Street was a landmark known around the world. This view was taken in the late 1860s. Courtesy, California State Library Collection, Sacramento Archives and Museum Collections Center

Facing page, bottom: During the 1850s and 1860s the city was periodically subjected to severe flooding. This lithograph shows the intersection of Front and J streets during the flood of 1850. The accuracy of this Casilear and Bainbridge print enabled renovators to authentically reconstruct several historic buildings. Courtesy, Sacramento Archives and Museum Collections Center

Below: The Central Pacific Railroad was built by scores of hardworking Chinese immigrants. In this 1867 photo laborers are seen constructing a trestle through the rugged Sierra Nevada Mountains. Courtesy, California State Library

arriving in San Francisco by the boatload, the pace of construction quickened. By the end of 1867, the CP had cleared the 7,047-foot summit of the Sierras. Fifteen months later, Leland Stanford drove the golden spike uniting the Central Pacific with the west-reaching Union Pacific at Promontory Point, Utah.

With its nearly dead-center location in the middle of California, both north-south and east-west, the Sacramento area expanded as a railroad center. Although riverboat steamers from the Gold Rush still shared in the transport trade from San Francisco up the Delta to Sacramento, the 1869 completion of the California Pacific line from Vallejo to Sacramento began cutting into their business. Additional lines through

Right: In 1903 the legislature purchased the Steffens/ Gallatin mansion at 16th and H streets for use as a governor's mansion. Built in 1877, the house was continuously used as a residence until the 1960s when Governor Reagan chose to live elsewhere. The site is now operated by the California Department of Parks and Recreation. Courtesy, Sacramento Housing and Redevelopment Agency Collection, Sacramento Archives and Museum Collections Center

Below: This view of the state capitol, taken about 1868, shows the brick construction technique, the incomplete dome, and an apse that was removed after World War II to make room for the East Annex. Courtesy, California Department of Parks and Recreation Collection, Sacramento Archives and Museum Collections Center

the foothills to the still-prosperous mines likewise eroded the monopoly once held (briefly) by the SVRR. And 18 miles east of Sacramento on oak-studded uplands, a new rail center was being born where the Central Pacific joined the California Central at the appropriately named town of Junction.

Sacramento in the Gaslight Era

By the 1870s, Sacramento, like the rest of the country, was immersed in the Industrial Age. The railroads were booming. The agricultural industry's regional hegemony was being challenged by manufacturing. Box factories, lumber mills, carriage builders, tanneries, and canneries were sprouting throughout the city, whose prominence in the state was matched only by San Francisco and Oakland. Indicative of its status, the state legislature chose Sacramento as California's capital after a bitter fight with rival cities Benicia, San Jose, Monterey, San Francisco, and Los Angeles. Begun in 1863, by the end of the decade the $2-million

The Gong family of Marysville posed for a formal portrait probably around the turn of the century. The sophisticated level of culture indicated by Chinese Americans' dress and attitude went unnoticed by the "pure" Americans dominating the social structure. Courtesy, California State Library, Sacramento Archives and Museum Collections Center

state capitol had finally been completed.

If the Gold Rush period was Sacramento's first Golden Age, the Gaslight Era (1870-1900) represented a more refined period. Consolidating its gains from mining, agriculture, transportation, and mercantile industries, the edifices constructed during the Gaslight Era offered florid testament to Sacramento's growing wealth and power.

Besides the Greek Classical Revival bronze-domed capitol at 10th and M streets, there was Pythian Castle, the turreted sandstone lodge of the Knights of Pythias, at the corner of 9th and I streets, and over on 5th and G, the Italianate *campanilles* of the Central Pacific station seemed to float over elm-arbored H Street, a street of palatial dwellings where Sacramento's silk stockings lived.

Of the H Street palaces, none was more grand than the Gallatin Mansion. Designed by N.D. Goodell and built by Uriah Reese for local merchant Albert Gallatin in 1877, the ornate ice-cream-white Victorian at the corner of 16th and H streets featured marble fireplaces, frescoed ceilings, and oak floors inlaid with mahogany and cherry. The Gallatin Mansion was the talk of the town, and the question on most Sacramentans' lips was how much did this monument cost? According to Lincoln Steffens, the muckraking journalist whose father later bought the house from Gallatin: "I recall only what my father said Mr. Gallatin told him, which was that he stopped counting when it got to Seventy-five thousand dollars."

The building remained a private residence until 1903, when the state bought it for the fire sale price of $32,500 and turned it into the official Governor's Mansion.

The Second Great Boom and the Immigrant Wave

Between 1870 and 1900, Sacramento experienced one of the major booms that have characterized its history from the beginning. In 1870, the population was 16,283. By 1900, it had soared to more than 29,000.

The growth of the railroad industry certainly helped spur the explosion; by 1900, over 2,500 workers were employed by the railroads, most of them by the Southern Pacific, the company that began merging with Central Pacific in the 1880s.

But at least equally important to the city's growth was the rise of the agricultural industry. By the 1870s, California had become the second-largest wheat-producing state in the nation. But as the century neared its end, fruits and vegetables began to overtake wheat, barley, and other grains in importance.

Most of the fruit and vegetable growers in the Sacramento area were located down the Delta in rural communities that had been reclaimed from winter floodwaters through levee building. The fruit and vegetable farms tended to be smaller and less mechanized than the vast wheat farms upriver. They also tended to be worked by the immigrant Chinese who built the railroads and levees and stayed on to settle in small Delta towns like Walnut Grove, Isleton, and Rio Vista.

More than any other racial or ethnic group, the Chinese were most responsible for ensuring the continued livelihood of the Sacramento region. Judah and The Big Four might have brainstormed and financed the railroad, but the Chinese built it. The big downriver farmers might have advanced the idea of levee building, but when it came to muscle, the Chinese supplied it. Regrettably, the state which once beseeched their arrival to help secure its future now turned viciously against the Chinese.

In 1886, Sacramento hosted an anti-Chinese convention, and by the 1890s anti-Chinese riots had become commonplace. Exclusionary laws forbidding the employment of Chinese were passed by federal, state, and local governments. The Chinese were vilified and spat upon, their settlements put to the torch.

But down in the Delta, the Chinese community luckily escaped the worst of these hateful persecutions. Although restrictive national immigration policies stopped the flow of further Chinese immigration to the Delta, those who were already here were allowed to live in relative if uneasy peace.

While Chinese immigration to Sacramento slowed, other ethnic groups continued to arrive in wave after wave. The German and Irish settlers, who arrived during the Gold Rush and were the first significant ethnic populations in Sacramento, were joined by their families, friends, and relatives during the Gaslight Era. In 1865, Peter Kunz, a nurseryman, established the Empire Nursery, the first wholly-owned German business in Sacramento.

But what Sacramento's German immigrants were best at was brewing beer. And in the spring of 1889, a trio of German *braumeisters*—Philip Scheld, Henry Grau, and Fred Ruhstaller—established the largest brewery west of the Mississippi.

Located at the crest of Poverty Ridge on 21st and R streets, the Buffalo Brewery was a five-story brick structure with mansard roofs and adjoining outbuildings with a total floor space of more than 50,000 square feet. Built for $400,000, the Buffalo Brewery had a capacity of 60,000 barrels a day and employed more than 150 workers.

Much of the brick that went into building the Buffalo Brewery was supplied by another of Sacramento's diverse ethnic groups, the Portuguese.

In 1860, there were 45 Portuguese immigrants in Sacramento—44 men and 1 woman. But by 1920, the number

Above: The novelty of cheap electricity led to excessive displays such as this one. On September 9, 1895, the 45th anniversary of California's admission day, the "Grand Electrical Carnival" lit up John Breuner's furniture company building at 6th and K streets. Other prominent city buildings, including the capitol, were also illuminated. Courtesy, Sacramento City Library, Sacramento Archives and Museum Collections Center

Facing page: The Capital City Wheelmen Racing Team, shown here, was the state champion for the 1903-1904 season. The Wheelmen also lobbied for road surface improvements. Courtesy, Sacramento City-County Library Collection, Sacramento Archives and Museum Collections Center

had grown to 572. Most of the Portuguese were from the Azore Islands, and the name of the district they occupied in Sacramento (between 5th and 10th streets south of R) was a bastardized derivation of their point of origin: locals called it the Arizona District.

Those Portuguese who didn't live in the Arizona District settled down the river in what came to be known as "The Pocket Area," where the Sacramento River formed a pocket by turning west and then southeast from its predominantly north-south course. Most of those living in the Pocket were employed as brickmakers at the Brickyard, the manufacturing plant they assembled at the point where the river made its turn west.

Other ethnic groups who would add to Sacramento's rich cultural heritage were likewise arriving as the nineteenth century entered its last quarter. Across the Sacramento River from the state capitol in what was the Gold Rush town of Washington (since renamed Bryte), a Russian colony was established. The Italian neighborhood was located in what would later be known as Alkali Flat. The Japanese immigrants occupied the area northwest of the Arizona District; the Croatians lived to the east.

Electric Rail and Electric Light

By the 1880s, some Sacramentans were already using Alexander Graham Bell's newfangled invention—"the talking box," or telephone. Electric rail lines, whose horse-drawn trolley predecessors had been running in Sacramento since the 1870s, crisscrossed the entire city by the late 1880s. (The competition between the competing streetcars was so fierce that the city eventually had to pass an ordinance prohibiting motormen from racing each other along parallel spurs.) As a mark of further civility, in 1890, the city of Sacramento installed concrete sidewalks, asphalt

streets, and a new water system.

But the most significant technological advance Sacramento experienced during the boisterous Gaslight Era was that which effectively marked the period's end. That came—or went—with the arrival of hydroelectric power in 1895.

The first electric lights had made their appearance in Sacramento as early as 1879. But until the arrival of hydro, most electrical production was reserved for either commercial uses or special displays like the annual state fairs held at Exhibition Park just east of Capitol Park.

The man most responsible for bringing hydroelectric power to the Sacramento area was the fabulously wealthy Horatio Gates Livermore, owner of the Natoma Water and Mining Company in Folsom. Livermore had a dream: dam the American River at Folsom, install turbines in a specially constructed power station, and transmit the electricity they generated through power lines strung the 22 miles between Folsom and Sacramento.

Working in partnership with Albert Gallatin and the General Electric Company, Livermore's dream became reality on July 13, 1895, when the nation's first water-powered, three-phase alternating current electricity was successfully transmitted from Folsom to Sacramento.

Less than two months later, on Admission Day, September 9, 1895, Sacramento celebrated its new hydro power with perhaps the greatest party the city had ever seen. During the week-long Carnival Of Lights, the estimated number of visitors taking part in the colorful citywide celebration exceeded 40,000, a number about one-and-a-half times greater than the entire population of Sacramento at that time.

By century's close, the original rectilinear grid of the city laid out by Warner and Sherman had been almost entirely built out, from Front Street on the waterfront to 31st Street at the eastern edge, and from Sutter's original landing on the American River at B Street to Y Street in the south. The city's cheap electric power was attracting new industries. The railroads were planning further expansions. The state government was growing. The fuse was lit for another period of explosive growth.

High Times

Pinpointing just what it was that sparked Sacramento's third major boom period is somewhat open to speculation. Certainly railroads, government growth, improved agricultural technology, and cheap electric power played a part, as did the booming national economy which shot through the roof as America became an international colonial power

Above: On December 15, 1935, the Tower Bridge across the Sacramento River at M Street was opened to the public. This concrete-and-metal structure has become a symbol of Sacramento. This photograph shows the procession that marked the bridge's opening. Courtesy, Caltrans, Sacramento Archives and Museum Collections Center

Facing page: Troops from Mather Field lined up at the rear of the old post office at 7th and K streets to escort the payroll to the Army Air Corps training base in 1918. The transportation of such large sums of cash always required protection. Courtesy, Eleanor McClatchy Collection, Sacramento Archives and Museum Collections Center

with its victory over Spain in the Spanish-American War. Perhaps it was partly due to something more ephemeral: faith in a future of seemingly limitless horizons.

Whatever the cause of the boom, Sacramentans could not dispute it once it descended on them. Between 1900 and 1910, the population increased from 29,282 to 45,000. In 20 more years it would double to 90,000. The economic evidence was even more compelling: between 1902 and 1914, the city's assessed real estate valuations soared nearly 400 percent from $17.6 million to $68.5 million. Bank clearings accelerated by 250 percent. Deposits increased 300 percent. Assets went up 400 percent. The city was both populous *and* wealthy. But there was no room left in the grid to accommodate the new arrivals. The city had to expand. So expand it did.

Oak Park, the city's first subdivision (built in the 1880s), was officially annexed in 1911. Additional outlying areas were likewise annexed, tripling the city's land area. Included in the annexation were Highland Manor, the subdivision south of Y Street, and other suburban areas east of town. A new form of transportation—the automobile—further accelerated Sacramento's radial expansion outward.

Even the little town of Junction was booming. Incorporated as the City of Roseville in 1907, the oak-studded plains were now dominated by the massive switching station Southern Pacific had built there in 1906.

Prosperity continued in Sacramento throughout the dinning teens and roaring twenties. It was the dawn of the Automobile Age, and the newly formed State Highway Commission was charged with integrating this new mode into Sacramento's varied transportation mix. Bridges to accommodate the auto were built across the American River. Roads were extended into the Sierras. In 1916, a causeway was built across the Yolo bypass, until then an impassable lake whenever winter or spring flooding occurred. Overland stages now competed with rail for passengers, if not yet for freight. But that was coming. The Highway Commission had plans for extending routes throughout Northern California, and Sacramento was ticketed as the system's hub.

The First World War brought the first military industry to Sacramento when Mather Field was built along a stretch of the American River seven miles east of the City of Sacramento. (Built in 1918, Mather's mission was the training of pilots and navigators.) The war also provided a shot in the arm to agriculture: between 1909 and 1919, local wheat sales jumped from $6.3 million to $36.9 million; vegetable revenues went from $12.1 million to $47.4 million; fruit and nut sales climbed from $50.7 million to $270.4 million.

As the twenties came to a close, Sacramento spent some of its wealth on municipal improvements, building two New York-style skyscrapers— The Elks Building and "the 926"—on busy J Street. In 1927, a building of similar Romanesque Revival design, the new 3,200-seat Memorial Auditorium, went up just down the street at the corner of 15th and J. And every evening at 6:00 when downtown workers left their offices, the Auditorium's chimes saluted their industry by playing "The Star Spangled Banner."

The Depression

By the 1930s that rousing salute had given way to the dirge whose overture was sounded on "Black Thursday," October 29, 1929. The Depression was upon Sacramento. The Embarcadero area by Front Street where the city had begun, and which had been gradually declining since the turn of the century when the city center began moving east, was now sliding further into decay. As the Embarcadero slid, the rooms of its old ornate hotels left over from the Gold Rush began filling up with migrant farm workers seeking work in the fields.

But the agricultural industry was as hard hit as big business was. Between 1919 and 1930, fruit and nut prices fell 22 percent; wheat prices dropped a whopping 300 percent. Only vegetable revenues remained stable. With agriculture prices falling faster than a barometer in a hurricane, Delta towns like the Chinese community of Locke all but dried up and blew away.

Sacramento's industrial production declined. Businesses failed. "Hoovervilles" sprouted up along the riverbanks. There were 27,000 unemployed workers in the County of Sacramento out of a total population of 250,000. The only local industry which remained relatively immune to the paralyzing blow of the Depression were the government industries whose charge it now was to try and rebuild the economy.

Franklin Delano Roosevelt's New Deal couldn't accomplish its stated goal of full employment for all Americans. But what a WPA and AAA couldn't do, a World War II could.

Expanding Military and Suburban Development

During the Second World War and its aftermath the military and its affiliated industries became major economic forces in the Sacramento area. Just as the First World War had brought Mather Field to the city, the subsequent war brought Sacramento two more military bases: McClellan Air Force Base in the North Highlands area of the city, and the Army Signal Depot, located east of town on the sandy plains of the old alluvial fan of the American River. Between them, McClellan and the Signal Depot employed almost 20,000 military and civilian workers; another 5,000 Sacramentans worked at Mather.

After the war, all three bases remained operative, employing large numbers of Sacramentans. (Depending upon whether the military economy was in a peacetime or wartime mode, the number fluctuated between 11,000 and 25,000.) The military bases were soon joined by another branch of the newly emerging military-industrial complex when Aerojet General Corporation established its rocket assembly plant in eastern Sacramento County.

And soon another boom was rumbling through Sacramento.

The returning veterans who started the postwar baby boom also inspired the suburban building boom, a phenomenon that swept the Sacramento area like a summer brushfire. Formerly independent communities and townships like Florin to the south, Perkins to the southeast, Carmichael and Fair Oaks to the east, and Citrus Heights to the northeast were now absorbed into the greater metropolitan area.

Above: The depression hit Sacramento hard. This 1930s photo shows a resident of "Hobo Jungle," a community of unemployed workers who occupied makeshift huts along the Sacramento River. Courtesy, Sacramento Archives and Museum Collections Center

Facing page: During the late 1970s, scaffolding, ladders, and metal bracing were familiar sights at the State Capitol Restoration Project. One of the largest restoration projects ever undertaken, it cost more than $60 million. The six-year project began in 1976 and was completed in January 1982. Courtesy, Elk Grove Citizen, photograph by DB Malloy

Highways were displaced by larger freeways, creating further development. Between 1955 and 1970, the population in the city soared from 138,000 to 263,000. During the same period, the population in Sacramento County zoomed from 346,000 to 650,000. Now the metropolitan area reached nearly to Folsom and Roseville.

Indicative of how potent an economic force suburbia had become was the fact that by 1963 the building trades industry equalled the transportation industry in Sacramento, each numbering 19,000 employees.

But those numbers paled in comparison to the burgeoning, so-called "recession-proof" government industry, which in 1963 employed 62,000 employees, comprising 31 percent of the local work force.

To make room for the commercial requirements of the ever-expanding state and federal governments—and as a way of dealing with the dreadful eyesore the Embarcadero area had become by then—in 1950 the City of Sacramento launched a major redevelopment project for the area between Front and Seventh streets from I to Q streets, sparing only the most historically significant buildings from slum clearance.

Sacramento's rapid expansion and the concomitant rise of suburban shopping malls created a corresponding negative effect on downtown retail, as did the decision to turn K Street, the retail center of downtown, into a pedestrian mall; with its uplifted concrete slabs (supposedly representing the nearby Sierras) actually impeding pedestrian access, critics came to refer to K Street as "the tank traps."

Then the recession of 1978-1979 dealt a crippling blow to the building trades industry. And the city adopted a slow-growth policy, creating a vacuum the more aggressively expansionist county government was all too ready to fill. Conflicts developed over where metropolitan Sacramento was heading and what course it should take to get there.

Though the disputes were often bitter, the various conflicts which erupted—between slow-growth, no-growth, and full-speed-ahead proponents, between city and county, and between the county of Sacramento and neighboring south Placer and El Dorado counties—eventually resolved themselves to the collective good of metropolitan Sacramento.

Gearing Up Again

It took some losses for Sacramento to realize that what was at stake was worth fighting for. It took bruising battles pitting the environmentalists against the developers to illustrate more could be gained from accommodation than acrimony. Sacramento would have to lose some of its Embarcadero and the Alhambra, its showplace moviehouse whose Moorish architecture was a mirror copy of the Alhambra in Granada, Spain. But it wouldn't allow the Memorial Auditorium to be torn down. And when a plan was put forward to raze the state capitol and replace it with two steel-and-glass towers, preservationists soundly defeated the proposal.

It cost $65 million to renovate the state capitol—33 times what it first cost to build it. But when its grand reopening was held on an icy winter night in early 1982, the 50,000 Sacramentans who turned out for the event beheld a spectacle that rivaled the 1895 Carnival of Light. Laser beams washed over the blindingly white facade. Music filled the streets. Fireworks seemed to explode from the

dome itself. The painstakingly restored capitol building gave Sacramentans a focal point for civic pride, and that feeling was growing as additional evidence of a metropolis regaining its bearings began manifesting itself throughout the region.

Downtown, a major commercial building boom was in progress. The capitol dome and the spires of the Cathedral of the Blessed Sacrament and the Elks and "926 J" buildings which once dominated the skyline are now themselves dominated by the 28-story Renaissance Towers and the Hyatt Hotel on Capitol Park. And downtown retail is back on the upswing.

A $176-million, 15-mile light rail line established in 1987 now carries commuters and shoppers downtown, and the Sacramento Regional Transit Board has announced plans to expand the system in the next five years.

Up in the foothills around Roseville, high-tech plants like Hewlett-Packard, INTEL, Avantek, and NEC are blooming and expanding like Southern Pacific once did at the turn of the century. In the decade between 1978 and 1988, high-tech employment shot up from 3,400 to 12,000. That number is expected to increase tenfold—to 120,000—by the end of the century.

While they're enthusiastic about the benefits economic expansion and diversification will bring, Sacramentans are eager to preserve the quality of life which has attracted new arrivals—residents and business—ever since the city began 150 years ago. Currently the city and county are considering development alternatives to the tradi-

tional suburban model which will have positive impacts on air quality and traffic. One such model, the high-density, mixed-use "pedestrian pocket," has received widespread support. Essentially a Europeanized variation of the nineteenth-century American township, the first pedestrian pocket in America will be constructed in south Sacramento County in the new Laguna Creek Estates development.

In another historical first, Sacramento also recently became the first community in the nation to shut down a nuclear power plant when voters cast a resounding "no" to Rancho Seco, the troubled nuclear-fired generating plant in the southeast county. Almost since its 1974 inauguration, Rancho Seco had been plagued by equipment failures and emergency shutdowns, and its continued operation had been locally debated for years. Though two previous efforts to close the plant proved unsuccessful, on June 6, 1989, Sacramentans voted to shut down Rancho Seco permanently.

The loss of Rancho Seco notwithstanding, there is an energized feeling in the air of this metropolitan area of 1.5 million people in the heart of the Great Valley. The mood is upbeat in the old Alcalde's former settlement: the economic future is promising, the citizenry passionately involved. As it once was during the Gold Rush, Sacramento is again booming and bristling with excitement. Now the fastest-growing metropolitan area in the nation, the once-sleepy river town state capital slumbers no longer.

Downtown Renaissance: The Grid Grows Up

Downtown: A Bird's Eye View
Smack in the middle of Sacramento, in the heart of a park filled with tall, shady trees gathered from all over the world, the copper-plated dome of the California State Capitol seems almost to hover, a gold globe above a sea of green. This is the nerve center of the state and the city, and from this stately hub, downtown Sacramento radiates outward.

Ten blocks to the west, the wide, green waters of the Sacramento River roll past the Gold Rush facades of Old Sacramento on their slow march south to the Delta. Fourteen blocks east of Capitol Park's manicured lawns, and past the Business 80 freeway, Alhambra Boulevard marks downtown's eastern border. Ten blocks north, behind earthen levee walls, the swiftly flowing American River rushes toward its confluence with the Sacramento at Discovery Park. Nine blocks south of the capitol, where Business 80 loops toward San Francisco, is the final line of demarcation in the city's central core. Anywhere within these borders is downtown Sacramento—what locals affectionately call "The Grid."

The term is derived from the gridlike system Captain W.H. Warner used to lay out the city of Sacramento in 1849: the regularly spaced, tree-canopied boulevards running north-south are the numbered streets; those flowing on east-west axes are denoted by letters. It's a system so simple even elementary schoolchildren can use it with ease.

Today, downtown Sacramento is a bustling hive of gleaming tower blocks interspersed with architecturally noteworthy Victorian mansions from the Gaslight Era and elegant apartment complexes from the 1920s. The capitol, once the tallest building downtown, is now dwarfed by adjacent neighbors like the Hyatt Regency Hotel, the Renaissance Tower, and the Central Library complex—structures all built during the booming 1980s. The ever-rising skyline and the quickstep of downtown

Older, traditional architecture is framed by the dynamic lines of contemporary sculpture in this view of the 1895 Elk's Lodge on J Street. Photo by Bob Rowan/Progressive Image Photography

development lend the city an air of cosmopolitan elegance and assuredness. But downtown Sacramento wasn't always so assured. In fact, when the city was founded after the Gold Rush, the prevailing fear was that Sacramento might not be able to survive at all.

Downtown Redevelopment of the 1950s

Downtown Sacramento eventually triumphed over the elements which threatened it during its early years—the winter floods and summer fires that followed an almost clockwork cycle. The city grew and prospered. Then, a century later, it was threatened again. This time the corrosive element was more sociological than elemental. Its name was urban blight.

By the 1920s the city center had shifted, moving eastward to the area around the state capitol where the new state treasurer's office and state supreme court buildings had recently been completed. The two new Greek Revival

Left: Four-and-a-half acres along the old Sacramento waterfront have been reconstructed to recall the days when steamboats and sailing vessels were moored along the river's edge. Photo by Tom Myers

Facing page, top: Replicas of gas lamps are among the careful details that help create Old Town Sacramento's authentic ambience. Photo by Tom Myers

Facing page, bottom: People visit Old Town Sacramento to enjoy its nineteenth-century waterfront flavor and to sample the latest California Pacific cuisine at eateries such as California Fats. Photo by Cathy Kelly Architectural Photography, courtesy, John F. Otto, Inc.

structures framed the fountained court on Capitol Avenue between 9th and 10th streets, an informal declaration that Sacramento's economy had moved from gold to government. And by this time, Captain Warner's grid had been completely built out and occupied, prompting the city to expand to suburbs in the north and south. These developments, coupled with the onset of the Depression, caused the old city center located along the Embarcadero to begin a long slow slide into urban decay.

Between 1937 and 1951, the assessed property in the west end—a 62-square-block, 242-acre, stairstep-shaped area between Front and 10th and I and R streets—had decreased by one-third in value. The streets which gold once raised and paved were now crowded avenues of human misery and despair. In 1951, the median income of west end residents was but $1,662 a year.

Though the district bordering the waterfront only comprised 8 percent of the city's total area, it held 20 percent of its population—most of them poor and unemployed transients. Those who held jobs were mostly employed as migrant laborers, or, as a 1954 *Architectural Digest* article termed it, "floaters on the day-rate labor sea." They occupied rooms in once-fashionable hostelries like the Orleans House and the City Hotel, which had since degenerated into flophouses, breeding grounds of crime and disease. A 1951 article in the *Sacramento Union* described the west end: "The area [is] a hodgepodge of cafeterias, employment agencies, pawn shops, public lockers, barber shops, bars, substandard housing and human breakdowns which result from slum conditions." Newspapers ran exposés of its hellhole habitations, ill health, and human degeneracy, and they began calling for remedial action.

By the early 1950s, Sacramento embarked on yet another massive public works project to salvage what it could of the waterfront district and preserve those build-

ings from its rich history.

What was wanted was then called "urban renewal." An agency—the Sacramento Housing Agency (later the Housing and Redevelopment Agency)—was formed to tackle the problem of how to effect this in the west end.

Starting in January 1951 with a loan of $6,394 from the city council, the five-member agency board put together a three-month budget to conduct a socio-economic survey of the city's west end.

The first thing the city should do, recommended the study, was buy the property in the west end. The cost was estimated at $12.5 million. The resale value was only $6 million.

But under a formula worked out with the federal government, which agreed to absorb two-thirds of the total $6 million loss, the city would be left with a net loss of only

$2 million. The city could recoup this loss by encouraging new development in the district, which it would designate a historic area.

The study said Sacramento should attempt to preserve as much of the west end as possible. The rest of it would be consigned to slum clearance.

A strong congressional lobby headed by Sacramento's Democratic Congressman John Moss secured additional federal funds to assist the west end's transformation. (Sacramento remembered Moss' help by naming its Capitol Mall federal building after him.) The first actual project, in 1952, was a modest two-square-block redevelopment opposite the Southern Pacific depot between 3rd and 5th and I and J streets, an office complex that later became Sacramento's Chinatown. The next project occurred between 1954 and 1960 when the gateway of Capitol Mall was created to displace what had been the city's "red light" district.

Additional slum clearance was accomplished by the controversial decision to route Interstate 5 through the heart of the old Gold Rush district. Although two alternate freeway routings were considered, in the end, the city regarded the west end routing as a way of killing two birds with one stone: it provided a throughway route for north-south interstate traffic and also cleared away some of the run-down district. Though many buildings of historical significance—like the old Wells Fargo pony express station and the first site of the *Sacramento Bee*—were lost to the wrecker's ball, enough buildings were preserved to begin turning the Embarcadero into a tourist-oriented "Old Town" section.

The first new business to locate in the six-block-square Old Town was The Firehouse restaurant. Built by San Francisco developer Ben Swig in the city's first firehouse, Swig's restaurant quickly became the restaurant where one went "to see and be seen," a favorite haunt of high-powered lobbyists, state legislators, and local bigwigs.

The massive redevelopment efforts helped reshape and reform the historical heart of the city. But downtown Sacramento wasn't entirely out of the woods, not by a long shot.

Downtown Turnaround in the 1980s
The cataclysmic changes that shook downtown in the

Above: Reflections of Capitol Mall architecture are seen in the windows of the Senator Salon, one of the many businesses that cater to Sacramento's public servants. Photo by Bob Rowan/Progressive Image Photography

Facing page: Restored to its original architectural grandeur in 1982, the California State Capitol, located at 10th and Capitol Park, is the elegant centerpiece of downtown Sacramento. Photos by Tom Myers

20-year period between the mid-1950s and mid-1970s also sent it into a traumatic shock, and it wasn't until the 1980s that Sacramento would fully recover from it.

By the mid-1970s, downtown Sacramento had become a modern-day ghost town: occupied from nine to five by state workers, all but deserted thereafter.

The state of drift downtown Sacramento fell into would only make the events of the 1980s more remarkable. Considering what had preceded it, the turnaround was just this side of a miracle.

Pinpointing the precise date when the turnaround began is a little difficult; the city seemed to shift from the doldrums into full-speed ahead as though its sails had suddenly filled with a strong tradewind. It's an apt metaphor, for it was the winds of trade itself that gave downtown renewed breath.

A trade organization formed in the mid-1970s played a key role. The Sacramento Area Commerce and Trade Organization, (SACTO) was established to attract investors back into the grid. John Roberts, SACTO's former president, says "What happened downtown was a good lesson for all of us. It showed what can happen when we neglect to take an active role and just let market forces overwhelm us. The decline of downtown didn't happen overnight, and neither did the turnaround. The turn-

was so much change occurring downtown that you needed a scorecard to keep track of it.

As seemed appropriate for the capital city, the first real evidence of a downtown renaissance was at the capitol itself. When a state engineer's report in the mid-1970s showed the century-old statehouse incapable of meeting earthquake code requirements, the legislature was faced with a difficult decision: tear down the old capitol and build a new one, or renovate what its occupants affectionately call "The Building."

The renovate or relocate debate expended a hot air balloon's worth of political wind, most of it coming from the late state senator Randolph Collier, who wanted to see twin tower blocks replace the old capitol. In the end, the

around can be summed up in one word: investment."

In the spring of 1983, a study was published on Sacramento's business outlook for the rest of the century. The report was titled "The Sanger Report," and what it projected for Sacramento was a future as rosy as the recent past had been bleak.

The projections in The Sanger Report (and other studies, like a Wharton econometrics study) showed Sacramento poised on the biggest boom it would see since the Gold Rush. The low cost of energy, available land, affordable housing, the healthy government economy, and a sunny projection for manufacturing jobs would create a period of strong and steady growth throughout the 1980s and into the next century, said the economic forecasters. Now was the time for downtown to begin making its move. It did so with a vengeance.

Reality followed the forecasts, and developers soon began buying up every available downtown lot, building, and lease. Where once there was only stasis, now there

Above: Officers of the California State Police provide security for the governor, patrolling the 40-acre park that surrounds the capitol. Photo by Bob Rowan/Progressive Image Photography

Right: This view of downtown Sacramento includes the Capitol Bank of Commerce (far right) and the Wells Fargo Center under construction to the bank's left. Photo by Bob Rowan/Progressive Image Photography

decision was made by then-Governor Edmund G. "Jerry" Brown, Jr., to restore The Building and make it *the* showpiece of downtown Sacramento.

It cost $2 million to build The Building. It took $65 million to rebuild it. The walls were earthquake-proofed. The legislative and executive chambers were refurbished. The rotunda was repainted in soft pastels and regilt in gold leaf at the crown. New mahogany staircases and 14-foot-tall arch-topped doors were replicated to conform with the original woodwork. The exterior was repainted a bright eggshell white and the six-story-tall dome was entirely recoppered.

On the cold, clear evening of January 3, 1982, The Building was unveiled to the public. As spotlights arced through the night sky, 15,000 Sacramentans converged upon Capitol Park to watch a spectacular laser light show and fireworks display celebrating the Capitol Restoration Gala. The weeklong gala served notice that downtown was back on track. Since then, the accumulated evidence has only underlined this fact.

A Rising Skyline

The next downtown shot-in-the-arm saw the beginning of a change in Sacramento's skyline, which has vaulted higher and higher since the 1980s. As in the early days of urban renewal, Capitol Mall served as the staging area.

In June 1984, Sacramento Mayor Ann Rudin turned the first spadeful of earth on a lot at the southeast corner of Third Street and Capitol Mall. Two years later, an 18-story, 300,000-square-foot office space occupied the lot and opened its doors for tenants. With its curvilinear bow-front facade and soft-green tinted windows, Sacramentans soon dispensed with the building's official name—the Capitol Bank of Commerce—and gave it a name of their own: "The Emerald Tower."

The Emerald Tower was a joint project built by the aforementioned Capitol Bank of Commerce and the RJB company, a development firm owned by Richard J. Benvenuti. Downtown development would soon become synonymous with the name Benvenuti.

Of the new major high rises built downtown during the 1980s, the Benvenuti family has had an interest in five of them, totaling 80 floors and some 4 million square feet of space. Headed by patriarch Joseph P. Benvenuti, the family has been one of the major players in recent Sacramento history—from their investment in the Sacramento Kings basketball team to the actual development of the 28-floor Renaissance Tower (Sacramento's tallest high rise, a title it will shortly relinquish).

Joe Benvenuti arrived in Sacramento in the late 1940s with $20,000 in savings from his days as a greengrocer in New Jersey. Shortly after coming to town, Joe became friends with Buzz Oates, a local developer who attended the same church. The two decided to become partners and began developing warehouses.

The money Joe Benvenuti made from produce was small potatoes compared to the fortune he derived from building concrete tilt-ups in Sacramento. Building warehouses may have allayed Joe Benvenuti's ambitions

for wealth but they didn't satisfy his spirit—not like building downtown monuments and sports palaces did. Soon the whole Benvenuti family was part of the act.

Following in Joe's footsteps, his son Richard also entered the development business, as did Joe's nephew and Richard's cousin, Danny. And in the 1980s, downtown Sacramento became, literally, a 'can you top this?' of one Benvenuti high rise after another.

The Benvenutis' contribution to the resurgence of downtown began with Richard's Emerald Tower/Capitol Bank of Commerce and continued with the $30-million, 380,000-square-foot Benvenuti Plaza mid-rise office complex at 15th Street along the new light rail line.

But the most visible Benvenuti monument downtown is the recently completed Renaissance Tower, the 28-floor, smoked-glass and marble-faced, ultramodern high rise located at the northeast corner of 8th Street and the K Street Mall. Opened in July 1989 at a festive gala attended by Sacramento's main movers and shakers, the $70-million, 341,000-square-foot building is visible from almost anywhere in the city. With its angular planes and dark blue glass panels joined by red granite trim, the Daniel, Mann, Johnson and Mendenhall-designed Renaissance is as sharp as the Capitol Bank of Commerce is soft. Characteristically, local Sacramentans have given the building a nickname: "The Darth Vader Building."

The Hyatt

In the spring of 1985, Joe Benvenuti announced he was entering into a partnership with developers Gregg Lukenbill and Bob Cook to build a new downtown hotel across the street from the Old Senator Hotel.

The Senator was emblematic of both downtown's boom and subsequent bust. Built in 1923, the Renaissance Revival Senator was the home away from home for powerful lobbyists and legislators during its heyday from the late

1930s to the late 1960s.

But by the 1960s, with California's rapid growth necessitating the need for a full-time legislature, the lobbyists and politicians who were the Senator's regular guests began seeking more permament lodgings. And, by then, downtown had become so dismal that the upscale hotel clientele began avoiding it altogether. Downtown's drift had claimed another victim.

In November 1983, the Senator changed ownership. The new owners decided to restore the building, but as politically oriented office space, not a hotel.

A similar fate befell the Hotel El Mirador. Located on the opposite side of Capitol Park (N Street), the El Mirador closed its doors as a hotel even earlier, in 1976, and was taken over by the Capitol Area Development Association. CADA used part of the 11-story building for its executive offices. The rest of the old El Mirador became a residence complex for senior citizens. By the time the Senator closed its doors, the only downtown hotel of note was the Holiday Inn, located on 5th Street at the west end of K Street Mall.

More than any other development, the $63-million Hyatt Hotel posed the question of whether a downtown renaissance was real or make-believe—people would come to work in downtown high rises, but would they stay in them?

Gregg Lukenbill believed they would.

Lukenbill wasn't just a developer, he was a promoter, some said a dreamer. Back in the mid-1970s, Lukenbill promised to bring major league sports to Sacramento. People shook their heads and laughed. But the brash young developer had the last laugh—all the way to the bank—when Sacramentans made his Kings a nightly sellout.

Almost singlehandedly Lukenbill brought the city its first major-league sports franchise. And it was Lukenbill, a Sacramento native, whose voice was loudest in urging his city to become what he called "a world-class city."

He lobbied the city council for help, and when that didn't work, he badgered it. He lost one partner in the hotel deal and then went out and got another. Eventually, he persuaded the city council into approving the Hyatt and giving him a subsidy to help build it. And though Sacramento would lose the lovely but decayed Francesca Apartments to make way for the Hyatt, Lukenbill's dream came true: he built it, and they came.

With its cream-colored facade, Memphis-influenced ironwork, and sloping teal roofs, the Hyatt has not only given Sacramento a first-class luxury hotel whose guests have included President Bush, but it has also brought class and elegance back to downtown. "Casual but sophisticated, that's the way I see us, and that's how I view this

city," says Morrie Graves, the Hyatt's general manager.

Directly opposite Capitol Park on L Street, and kitty-corner from the capitol, the Hyatt's 502 guest rooms and 30 luxury suites provide a dramatic setting for out-of-town guests and convention-goers. Twelve meeting rooms on the second floor provide 28,000 square feet of space, and the massive main ballroom can accommodate 1,800 guests. The walls and lobby are adorned with contemporary art from some of Sacramento's more noted artists and its three restaurants and lounges act as gathering spots for hotel guests and local Sacramentans out for a night on the town. Locals especially favor Busby Berkeley's, the lounge on the 15th (top) floor, where the jazz is hot and sweet and the view from the open air terraces spectacular.

The Urban Design Plan

Projects such as the Emerald Tower, the Hyatt Regency and the restored Capitol Building indicated that downtown development was an attractive proposition again. But each project was an end in itself, a stand-alone, case-by-case affair. That each project succeeded was more serendipitous than planned, a testament to their respective developers' faith in them and the healthy local economy rather than to a comprehensive plan for downtown development. That began to change when Sacramento instituted its Urban Design Plan.

The Urban Design Plan architects laid out planning concepts, development concepts, and design concepts. The total intent was to create a city center that worked, what the plan referred to as "a choreographed urban experience." The plan adopted streetscape standards to make downtown avenues more congenial through lighting, signage, landscaping, and pedestrian linkages. It created exacting design standards to give downtown a recognizable look and character. It suggested building types and spoke to the need for more public places.

One of the first things the plan did was dispense with height restrictions on downtown development, thereby encouraging an ever-rising skyline. The tallest high rises would be concentrated in the city's central core between the capitol and I-5 and City Hall on I Street in the north. The idea, according to senior city planner Gene Masuda, was "to create a tiered, wedding-cake effect with City Hall and Plaza Park at the center of it." The planners further sought to choreograph the urban experience by promoting healthy street life with everything from sidewalk cafes to outdoor events in public places to specified retail uses of ground floor spaces in anticipated new buildings. Now downtown development was less a hit-or-miss, hope-

for-the-best, roll of the dice and more a connect-the-specified-dots to achieve an integrated whole.

"Our intent was to give downtown both form and direction," says Masuda. "We all knew growth was coming—there was no way of avoiding it even if you wanted to, which we didn't. The Urban Design Plan was our way of taking the bull by the horns."

In February and again in June 1987, the city council adopted the Urban Design Plan and passed ordinances to ensure compliance with it. It was a significant achievement; after so long a struggle, direction had finally replaced drift. As Joe Serna, the most senior member of the Sacramento city council, put it, "For the first time in 20 years, I feel really optimistic about downtown revival. It's our cultural, civic, and corporate center, and now it's starting to reflect that again."

The effects of the Urban Design Plan are manifest throughout today's downtown Sacramento. Where winos once dominated Plaza Park, the old city square directly across from the Victorian baroque, white-on-white City Hall, now you'll find an open farmer's market on Wednesdays or open-air concerts during the jazz festival season in late May. The same holds true for other public spaces like St. Rose of Lima Park on K Street Mall. Downtown isn't just safe again, it's a fun place to be, and a great place to shop.

Light Rail and the Return of Retail
In 1985, the Sacramento city council decided to do away with the tank traps in an attempt to make K Street more accessible and hopefully lure shoppers to downtown again.

It was the beginning of K Street's metamorphosis. The city figured another way of getting those shoppers back on K Street was to give them direct access to it. The new light rail line would help do that.

On the last day of his term as transportation secretary in the Jimmy Carter administration, Neil Goldschmidt signed the authorization for release of Urban Mass Transit Authority funding to help build the first leg of a light rail system in Sacramento. In 1985, construction actually began on the $189-million, 18-mile, fishhook-shaped trolley line that paralleled Highway 50 east to the suburb of Rancho Cordova and then bent back around I-80 to the northeast through areas where Sacramento's suburban concentration and commuter traffic was heaviest. The curve of this fishhook was located on K Street.

More than any other downtown street, K Street was most affected by the drift of the 1960s and 1970s. Once Sacramento's prime shopping street, and the site of most of its movie theaters, the concrete tank traps might just as well have been quicksand as far as K Street retailers were concerned. When Weinstock's (formerly Weinstock-Lubin's, Sacramento's oldest department store established by David Lubin in 1924) closed its doors in 1980 at 12th and K and moved west to Dowtown Plaza, the last reigning symbol of K Street's consumer heyday was gone.

Light rail has helped bring it back. With ridership figures growing steadily—especially on weekends when more than 30,000 Sacramentans use it—downtown has once again become a shopper destination.

In the spring of 1989, the foot traffic of noontime shoppers, the increased volumes of ridership, and the downtown building boom prompted the city to unveil plans for a $90-million renovation of Downtown Plaza.

With 700,000 square feet of retail space, the Downtown Plaza was one of the biggest shopping malls in metropolitan Sacramento. It wasn't, however, one of the busiest. While shopping malls out in the suburbs like Sunrise, Birdcage, Florin, and Arden Fair grew in size and stature during downtown's drift, the plaza was hard-pressed to hold its own.

But by the end of the 1980s, the plaza too would begin to participate in the downtown renaissance.

Developer Ernest Hahn of San Diego, builder of that city's Horton Plaza, and architect Jon Jerde, who designed it, again joined forces to redo Downtown Plaza. Groundbreaking began in February 1990 on a million-plus-square-foot mall that will include a 25,000-square-foot food court, a 6- to 10-screen cinema complex, and a European-styled series of plazas and piazzas. "We think this is going to be an exciting addition to the downtown mix," says city planner Dick Hastings. "It'll be a great place to shop, eat, or just while away an hour with a friend over capuccinos."

Lot A: The Jewel in the Crown

Throughout 1989, Sacramentans would witness one of the most hotly contested and intriguing development battles the city had seen since the question of redevelopment was first debated back in the 1950s. Again, the Housing & Redevelopment Agency was at the center of the storm.

In the early 1980s, the very idea of development downtown was still being battled by environmental

Above: The raising of Sacramento's skyline continues at a fast pace. Seen here is the recently completed Lankford-Cook Building, located on the corner of 12th and K streets. Photo by Tom Myers

Facing page: K Street attractions such as the Crest Theater are easily accessible via Sacramento's convenient light rail system. Built in 1939, the theater was reopened in 1986 as a revival house. Photo by John Elk III

groups like the Environmental Council of Sacramento (ECOS) and the Sacramento Old City Association (SOCA), which tended to view it as a threat to older, established neighborhoods. But by the late eighties, when the idea of commercial development in the central business district had achieved legitimacy, the combatants in the battle had changed. ECOS and SOCA were still active participants in the struggle to preserve downtown neighborhoods like the Southside District and Alkali Flat as

residential neighborhoods. And environmental groups still question the wisdom of intense development in the R Street corridor, where a number of high-rise office buildings are currently under discussion. But local environmentalists are less inclined to fight the city on the high rises it wants built in the inner city. By the end of the eighties, the combatants were the developers themselves.

Such was the case with the battle for Lot A, the site of a city parking garage occupying a full block bordered by 6th and 7th streets and L Street and Capitol Mall. When the city decided to develop the site in late 1988, they entertained seven separate proposals from some of the world's most prestigious architects and development firms. The city wanted a landmark building on the site, and the devel-

opers began dreaming up ways to give them one.

The process took seven months to wind from short list to finalist, and the politicking was hot and heavy for what city councilwoman Kim Mueller calls "the crown jewel in downtown development."

The four finalists for the Lot A crown proposed developments that were priced at anywhere from $156 million to $241 million. Some proposals favored twin, or triple towers; others called for single towers. The shortest was projected at 34 stories; the tallest at 57. The projected revenue the city would receive from Lot A by 2010 ranged from $33 million to $68 million. The strain of the process began to take its toll. When Gregg Lukenbill questioned the city's demand that all bids include a 300-room luxury hotel within the development, the list

The Central Library Project

Peter McCuen, the former Stanford University engineering professor turned Sacramento developer, not only won the Lot A battle but was also awarded another major downtown project when the city chose him to develop the new Central Library project.

The Central Library project was a victory for both preservationists and commercial developers. Though handsome, the old, three-story central library, a brown sandstone edifice with lion's head bas-reliefs on the facade, was both undersized and in need of an upgrade. But with downtown land values rising to nearly $150 a square foot by the end of the 1980s, a mere refurbishment of the existing structure built in 1921 was an economically unsound proposition. McCuen's project accomplished a threefold objective. First, it preserved and expanded the library by increasing its capacity with a compatibly designed adjoining building. Then it tied the new expanded library into a 22-story, 435,000-square-foot office building. Finally, it also included a parking garage capable of accommodating 690 cars.

Approved in 1987, the Central Library project grew like Jack's beanstalk during construction. Originally planned as an 11-story structure, in the spring of 1988 the developers sought, and won, approval to increase the building height to 18 floors. In the summer of 1989, they again won a design review approval to raise the building height by another four floors. With an additional three-story mechanical penthouse, when it opens in the summer of 1991 the Central Library project will be only 20 feet shy of the Renaissance Tower in height.

Located on the block between 8th and 9th, and I and J streets, the Central Library project anchors the west end of Plaza Park. On the opposite side of the park, a new eight-story parking garage completes the Plaza Park enclosure.

And still, the raising of Sacramento's downtown skyline continues. The total square footage projections for major downtown office space in the sky-vaulting 1980s has been nothing short of astronomical—nearly 12 million square feet have either been built, planned, or are under construction. The

was reduced by one.

The redevelopment agency considered three factors when making its recommendations: revenue return to the city, design, and feasibility of performance. According to the agency, the best project was the $180-million, dual-towered (34 and 37 stories), 836,000-square-foot Lankford & Cook proposal.

But after laborious debate, and some 11th-hour delaying tactics on the part of Lot A losers, the city council went against the agency's recommendation and awarded the contract to Peter McCuen's team. The decision was controversial because it allowed McCuen to build the project in stages, the office tower first and the hotel later. The first phase is expected to be completed in 1992; the second phase in 1995.

Benvenutis have a new 400,000-square-foot high rise planned to replace the old Greyhound bus terminal at 7th & L streets. Wells Fargo is about to build a 500,000-square-foot office building on Capitol Mall. Directly adjacent to the 1215 K, Lankford-Cook is adding a 300,000-square-foot, mirror image of the original. New hotels are springing up. A 150-room Sheraton Hotel is under construction at 8th & 0 streets, and the long-delayed Docks Project, which combines a 245-room Embassy Suites Hotel with a 200-slip boat marina, has finally gotten underway just below the Tower Bridge at Capitol Mall and the Sacramento River.

Development Beyond the Central Core

Within the central business district, the area bounded by R, G, and 16th streets and I-5, high rises race toward the heavens. Building cranes whir overhead, and jackhammers and pneumatic riveters punctuate the human bustle. When he was executive director of the Housing and Redevelopment Agency, Andy Plescia said, "The sound of piles being driven into the ground was music to my ears," a succinct summation of what the 1980s were like in the central core.

But when you pass out of the CBD into the rest of downtown, you enter a different, quieter world. Di-

rectly north and south are the ethnic neighborhoods of Southside and Alkali Flat, where the music you'll hear is more likely salsa. Both neighborhoods, with their nineteenth-century Victorians, have been upgraded since the seventies. Some of the more spectacular homes have been renovated and reconverted from living quarters to professional offices housing attorneys, accountants, and associations. But much of Alkali Flat and the Southside retains its ethnic flavor. Still in transition, both are beginning to show signs of turn-around due largely to the healthy local economy.

Crossing 16th Street and heading east, one enters Midtown, Sacramento's most culturally diverse and outright colorful neighborhood.

Midtown is a mixture of *la vie boheme* and the *petit bourgeois,* a district of sidewalk cafes, chic boutiques, professional buildings, art galleries, and elegant restaurants like Harlow's Cafe and J.R.'s on J Street, Biba's on Capitol

Avenue, and N Street's Paragaray's and Capital Grill. Here, the mode of transit is usually by foot or bicycle, and the mood is more laid-back.

Which is not to say sleepy, not like it was in the seventies. Midtown's main shopping street, J Street, the former stage road to the gold fields up the American River, also reflects the eighties boom, and the upscale shops springing up along it have struck a rich ore of consumer gold. J Street shops like How Tacky, Art Related Things, and The Taylor's Art Complex cater to tastes that run the gamut from refined to funky. Steve Priley, co-owner of Java City and two other Midtown coffee bars that have largely contributed to its renaissance, puts it this way: "There's no other place on this planet that I'd rather be in business. You can sense something's happening down here. More than that, you can see it and feel it."

At the eastern edge of Midtown are three of the more architecturally interesting buildings built during the eighties. All constructed by Domich-Separovich, a local development firm, the Sutter Square Galleria retail center and the two Farmer's Market Place commercial buildings reflect a more futuristic vision for Sacramento. The multi-colored Galleria actually wraps around the Business-80 freeway, and the two Farmer's Market Place buildings, totaling nearly 600,000 square feet of commercial space, have introduced an element of industrial high-tech to Sacramento.

The Southern Pacific Depot

In the 1960s and 1970s, Sacramento lost far more battles to preserve its past than it won. The Alhambra Theater fell. So did more buildings from the Gold Rush in the west end, and many Victorians in Alkali Flat, the Southside, and Midtown. Some of it could be attributed to neglect. Some of it could be laid at the door of developers whose sense of civic responsibility was far less than their commitment to turning a quick buck. Maurice Read, who led the fight to save the Alhambra and is now spokesman for Gregg Lukenbill, puts it this way: "Not enough people got involved back then. And those of us who did were terribly naive about the realities of getting things done."

Happily, this is no longer the case in Sacramento. Successful battles have been waged downtown to preserve the Hastings Building, a home dating from 1861, and Mori's Place, a Victorian Mansion built in 1877 that later served as a mortuary (hence the waggish name), which is now in the process of being converted into a youth hostel.

Sacramento may embrace the futuristic, as Lot A, the 1215 K Building, and the Emerald Tower attest. But it has also come to value its past. The most shining example of this is the ongoing effort to restore the Southern Pacific depot.

From the SP site at 6th & H streets, the race to build a transcontinental railroad began in 1863. The present building, opened in 1926, succeeded three other such terminals.

An Italianate brick complex of buildings on a 36.5-acre site with

an adjoining 203 acres of land to the north of it, the SP yards once shepherded a train through Sacramento every 15 minutes. But when trains fell out of favor as a viable transportation mode, the depot fell eerily quiet, its 5,000 employees reduced by half.

After the city acquired the site from Southern Pacific, a nine-member panel headed off on a transcontinental tour to study similar renovated sites in Washington, D.C., Indianapolis, Baltimore, St. Louis, and Portland. Later that year, the city selected the design team of Roma and Associates to plan the site as a public attraction. Roma, a San Francisco firm whose reputation for pedestrian-oriented design was earned with its work on Portland's Riverview Place, San Francisco's northeast Marina, and Vancouver's Expo site, will attempt to bring a similar human-scaled, mixed-use development to Sacramento.

A Drift Past Today's Downtown

The most visible example of downtown Sacramento's renewal is told in concrete terms: high rises, hotels, and the renovation of its historic district. But sometimes it takes a symbol to thematically underscore what hard evidence tells us. Sometimes it's the subtler shadings that more clearly illuminate the whole.

To understand that downtown's drift has now been rendered a past chapter in the city's ongoing history, all one needs to do is take a boat, drift down the Sacramento on a summer's night, and look at the city's illuminated silhouette.

Facing page, top: Lit by neon, Rick's Dessert Diner on J Street is among the many popular eateries frequented by visitors to midtown. Photo by Tom Myers

Facing page, bottom: Caffe Donatello, a hot new restaurant located in Town and Country Village at the corner of Fulton and Marconi, offers Northern Italian fare in an elegant setting. Photo by Cathy Kelly Architectural Photography

Below: Spanning the Sacramento River, the Tower Bridge is seen here illuminated at night with the Capitol Bank in the background. Photo by George Elich

The brightest object that greets the eye is also one of the oldest. As you approach the esplanade of Capitol Mall, you pass directly under Tower Bridge, a lovely 737-foot span built in 1935 that ties Sacramento to West Sacramento. Once wreathed in fog and darkness, the bridge was fully lighted in the summer of 1989, largely due to the efforts of Sacramento County Supervisor Sandy Smoley. The lighting of Tower Bridge took only $250,000 to accomplish, a pittance compared to high rises and their hundred-million-dollar budgets.

Still, the bridge lighting, in its own way, is maybe the more resonant note in the decade-long movement of downtown's symphony of renewal. It is both symbol and metaphor, a beacon that calls both native and newly arrived Sacramentans. And as the current takes one past it, the light dancing off the river, even the most skeptical viewer can't help but marvel. More than a structure of architectural beauty, the Tower Bridge is a statement, an elegy to the past, a commentary on the present, and a counterpoint to what the future holds in store for Sacramento. Here is the gateway to a city poised on greatness, it says, a city that rose and fell, rose again, and rises still.

CHAPTER 3

From Gold to Grain to Government: An Evolving Economy

An Ever-Evolving Economy

Canadian urbanologist Jane Jacobs believes that all successful cities are characterized by two hallmarks: their capacity to replace imports of foreign goods and services, and their ability to improvise innovations to cope with situations brought on by development. If this is so, Sacramento can lay claim to such a title, for it has done just this from its Gold Rush beginnings all the way through its history.

From the Gold Rush to Sacramento's middle period, the Gaslight Era bridging the two centuries, the economy expanded and evolved. Though still a stronghold of the local economy, the mercantilism of the Gold Rush now tended to serve residents of the city instead of foothill miners. New manufacturing industries—lumber mills, box factories, and ironworks—went into production. The grain-based agricultural economy turned its energy to more profitable fruit production. Steamships and stages gave way to transcontinental trains and an extensive, early-day light rail system that tied all neighboring towns to the growing Sacramento metropolis. Where once all goods came around the Horn and then traveled up the Delta on steamboats and barges, now Sacramento produced what it needed. Importing gave way to exporting.

Sacramento's businesses and industries evolved still further during the teens and twenties of the new century. Government and newly located military industries displaced the mercantile economy to an even greater degree than had manufacturing. Canneries were now the kings of the local food production economy. Highways and cars pushed rail, trains, and trams aside as lynchpins in the local transportation industry.

The evolution of Sacramento's economy continued in the postwar period with the arrival of the aerospace industry

Since the 1940s, massive expansion of metropolitan Sacramento has created a booming construction industry. More than 24,000 Sacramentans currently work in building trades. Photo by Bob Rowan/Progressive Image Photography

Facing page, above, and right: Sacramento is a heartland community whose major crops include pears, almonds, and tomatoes. Photos by Tom Myers (facing page) and Mark Gibson (above and right)

Below right: Sheep graze within sight of Sacramento's downtown. Photo by Richard Kaylin

and the growth of the housing industry. New subdivisions popped up like mushrooms after a spring rain. And though the once-busy canneries ceased their clatter, agricultural co-ops like the rice and almond growers exchanges assumed leadership in Sacramento's food production chain. Government-oriented employment skyrocketed still faster, assuming the role of Sacramento's largest employer, a position formerly held by the railroads.

The tide of the local economy would shift again in the eighties when manufacturing turned from harder goods to high-tech industries, as the arrival of prestigious firms like Hewlett-Packard, INTEL, and NEC attested. After enduring a decade of cutbacks, aerospace would rebound. And the still-vigorous housing industry began exploring new options in the late 1980s to help enhance Sacramento's liveability. It moved away from sole reliance on single-family dwellings to a new concept called "pedestrian pocket" developments, a more environmentally sound suburban development which combines elements of nineteenth-century American towns with futuristic, high-density mini-cities.

Agriculture: The Historic Meal Ticket

The rich, black-soiled land of the valley—nutrient-rich from centuries of silt deposits borne by the crisscrossing rivers—surrounds the city of Sacramento and presents the eye with a seemingly endless vista of green. Gold may have put Sacramento on the map, but the richness of green—vegetables, grain, and fruit orchards—have been its perennial sustenance, as constant a part of Sacramento life as are its rivers.

In 1988, the amount of revenue Sacramento County derived from agriculture totalled some $195 million. Other industries, namely government, construction, and high tech, passed agriculture long ago in terms of economic prominence. But they have not dislodged it in a deeper, more spiritual sense. Its sophistication aside, Sacramento is a heartland community, and agriculture has played a preeminent part in forming the local character which might best be described as patient, watchful, and conservative—not in the political sense of the word, but in the frugal sense, as in a farmer's sense of conservancy.

In the beginning, it was field crops that were Sacramento's greatest agricultural asset—crops like wheat, hay, and barley. But by the late nineteenth century grain crops began giving way to orange and lemon groves and pear, peach, and almond orchards—cash crops perfectly suited to the long, regular growing seasons the Sacramento region enjoys. With its moderately wet winters, moist springs, hot summers, and mild autumn harvest seasons, the Sacramento Valley was made to order for fruit production.

Farmers were also attracted by fruit production's versatility. In wheat or barley production, fields were solely dedicated to one crop. But with fruit, farmers could rotate the fields to accommodate different varieties and their respective growing cycles.

Truck farmers sold the fruit whole, by bushel and basket at open markets like the old Farmer's Market at 30th and S streets. Then they discovered the benefits of canning, and an entire new phase of the agricultural industry arrived in Sacramento.

According to Sacramento historian Joseph McGowan, "canneries remade the face of the valley between 1890 and 1910 . . . They enabled farmers to make a living from thirty to fifty acres of fruit trees, when he could not live off six hundred or a thousand acres of wheat."

In January 1882, the first major cannery in Sacramento was established at the corner of Front and K streets. In the first year of production, the Capitol Packing Company's 400 workers canned 400 cases of fruit, honey, asparagus, and salmon. Others, like the Sacramento Drying and Canning Company, Hunt Brothers, and Libby, McNeil, and Libby likewise established canneries in Sacramento. Still others sprang up in nearby valley towns like Woodland, Marysville, and Yuba City.

During the early 1900s, advances in canning technology

Above: The Libby, McNeill, and Libby cannery is a good example of adaptive reuse. Closed in the mid-1960s, the building has now been converted into office space and a gym. Photo by Bob Rowan/Progressive Image Photography

Facing page: An integral part of Sacramento's economy, the California Almond Grower's Exchange occupies a national landmark building located beneath the American River levee. Photo by Richard Kaylin

and fruit yield production inspired the establishment of additional canneries in Sacramento. But by the 1920s, the industry had begun to fade. The establishment of the state highway system and the subsequent growth of automotive trucking caused the cannery industry to move away from railroad towns like Sacramento to Bay Area locations. And the orchards themselves were steadily absorbed by the growth of Sacramento suburbs.

Still, in the 1980s, fruit production remains a strong part of the local economy. In downriver Delta towns like Clarksburg, Hood, and Courtland, the pear and peach orchards are still the dominant agricultural force they once were. And in such towns, their riverfront warehouses lettered with painted advertisements faded by the sun, time seems to have stood still.

Though agricultural production in the Sacramento Valley crested in 1980, in 1988 fruit and nut crops were second only to field crops in terms of gross revenue in local farm commodities. By themselves, pears accounted for nearly half the $37 million of fruit and nut crop revenue. In 1988, 6,300 acres of pears under harvest in the Sacramento Valley yielded 132,000 tons of fruit worth nearly $21 million.

Almonds and Tomatoes: Agricultural Kings

Pears may be the top local grosser, but in recent years almonds have become the glamour crop in Sacramento's fruit and nut economy.

Between 1960 and 1987, the amount of almonds produced in California increased from 53 million to 680 million pounds. Acreage devoted to almond production has doubled and is still rising, exceeding other crops such as grapes, pears, citrus, and avocados in the amount of acreage under production. The vast majority of these almonds

are processed in Sacramento.

The home of California almonds is located in midtown Sacramento on a 90-acre, 33-square-block site just beneath the American River levee. Once the home of the Del Monte Packing Company, one of the last major canneries to locate in Sacramento, the site is now occupied by the California Almond Growers Exchange, otherwise known as the Blue Diamond Growers.

There are currently more than 5,000 members in the Almond Growers Exchange, which processes more than 60 percent of all the almonds grown nationally, sometimes as much as one million pounds a day. With assets totaling more than $200 million, a payroll of $50 million, and 3,000 employees at the height of the almond season (1,000 year-round), the Almond Growers Exchange is an integral part of the Sacramento economy.

"Just a can a week is all we ask," goes the award-winning Blue Diamond television spots featuring actual growers standing knee-deep in a warehouse full of almonds. According to *Advertising Age*, "This charming campaign, starring real California Blue Diamond almond growers, is another in a series of wonderful advertising from commodities groups."

The ads have been highly instrumental in promoting almond consumption, which ranks first nationally in all tree nuts consumed. Moreover, the ads established national awareness of Blue Diamond almonds, which now have an almost 95 percent share of all almonds stocked on grocery shelves.

Today, the Blue Diamond Almond Growers Exchange markets its nuts to 94 countries all over the world—from Argentina to Uganda, from Austria to Thailand, from Japan to the Soviet Union. In 1983, the exchange sent a million pounds of almonds to Algeria (the largest single

In addition to fruit and nuts, rice is one of the main-stays of the Sacramento region's economy. Photo by George Elich

movement of almonds ever shipped) for the Muslim Rama-dan Festival. The record didn't last long. In 1989, the So-viet Union broke it by importing a single shipment of 25.3 million pounds worth $20 million.

Sacramento visitors can see the almond operation in per-son by visiting the 250,000-square-foot plant, which has since been designated a national landmark. Visitors can sample some of the 2,000 almond-derived products at the Visitors Center, and the tour has become a favorite destina-tion point for Sacramento visitors.

Besides fruit and nuts, the Sacramento region's agricul-tural economy is also founded on a number of other com-modities which help explain its nickname as "breadbasket of the world": sugarbeets and sweet corn, walnuts and grapes, asparagus and alfalfa, and a cornucopia of fruits, grains, and vegetables.

During the Nixon era of *detente* when the United States begin selling vast amounts of wheat to the Soviet Union, this commodity, once the king crop in Sacramento's local farm economy, began rebounding. In 1964, the wheat market brought local farmers only $750,000. But by 1980, local wheat sales had zoomed to nearly $23 million.

Other local farm commodities, especially rice, saw vast increases in production. Between 1950 and 1984, rice produc-tion doubled, and sales increased by 600 percent.

But rather than fruits, nuts, or grain, the food item that in many ways symbolizes Sacramento is the humble tomato. In fact, one of Sacramento's nicknames is "the Big Toma-to," or, better yet, "Sacratomato."

In one respect, it's somewhat undeserved; the amount of local tomato acreage has actually decreased by half over the past 30 years. Be that as it may, the only other symbol that comes close to typifying Sacramento for locals is the camellia, the flower that graces the official city logo.

When the Libby, McNeill, and Libby cannery closed its doors in the mid-1960s, Campbell's Soup was left as the last Sacramento tomato canner still in operation, a distinc-tion it still holds.

Located on a 136-acre site in South Sacramento, the light green Campbell's soup complex is a landmark of the city's south side. Campbell's Soup is one of Sacramento's largest employers with 1,700 full-time workers augmented by another 300 seasonal workers during the tomato season,

which runs from early July to mid-October. Built in 1947, the plant has a total of 1.25 million square feet of build-ings and an annual payroll of $50 million.

Besides tomato paste and other tomato products, like Prego spaghetti sauce, the plant also turns out everything from the famous soups to pitted olives to salad dressings—a total of 35 million cases of food a year.

According to plant manufacturing manager Steve Wright, the biggest change at Campbell's in the past 10 years isn't so much technological as it is philosophical.

Taking a page from the management manuals of Japanese companies, Campbell's Soup instituted a program called "quality circles," which gives employees greater control over their particular areas of expertise. "We realized that our people were our most important asset," Wright says, "and so we set up this program to capitalize on that. They're responsible for production within their own lines and on the products those lines produce. When they have a problem, they take care of it internally."

The Port of Sacramento: Link to the Ocean
When all those millions of pounds of almonds are packed and cased and readied for shipment to foreign markets, many of them begin their journey with a short jaunt across the Sacramento River to the city of West Sacramento, where the Port of Sacramento is located.

During the Gold Rush and all through the nineteenth century, the Port of Sacramento was located along the Embarcadero in what is now Old Town. But river transportation was all but rendered obsolete by the advent of the

Right: The red-and-white logo is a distinguishing feature of the Campbell's Soup plant in South Sacramento. The company is one of the area's largest employers with 1,700 full-time workers. Photo by Richard Kaylin

Facing page: At the Port of Sacramento a conveyor belt system elevates woodchips into a pile, readying them for storage prior to shipment to Japan for use in paper products. Photo by Mark Gibson

Below: With a $76-million channel deepening scheduled for completion in 1997, the Port of Sacramento is expected to become an attractive alternative to more expensive San Francisco Bay area ports. Photo by George Elich

railroads and then trucking.

Then, in the 1930s, Sacramento began considering the river as a transportation option again. The problem was that the river wasn't deep enough to handle modern ship traffic. The Second World War interrupted plans to deepen the Sacramento's channel, but by 1949 the Army Corps of Engineers had begun dredging the river and digging a new channel across previously dry land. This "deep water channel" runs from Collinsville on the Sacramento River nearly 43 miles to the port.

In 1963, the Army Corps of Engineers had finally completed the monumental task of dredging, deepening, and rerouting the channel. And on June 29 of that year, the *Taipei Victory* became the first ship to be received at the new Port of Sacramento.

Shipping increased steadily during the port's first 17 years of operation. Besides almonds, the main cargoes shipped by the port included logs, paper pulp and wood chips, rice and wheat, and other agricultural products. The main imports were fertilizer (imported for agribusiness) and newsprint. Arriving in Sacramento from plants in Sweden and Norway, Sacramentans thumb that newsprint daily when reading the *Sacramento Bee*. (Half of the newsprint the *Bee* uses is derived from these sources.)

In the 1980s, a worldwide adjustment occurred in the economy that seriously cut into the port's trade. Importing countries like Taiwan and Korea began turning to native production of commodities like rice and were soon exporting it themselves. Additionally, the onset of paper recycling in Japan resulted in a concommitant reduction of wood chip exports. Furthermore, the shipping industry's move toward larger container ships and tankers seriously cut into the amount of tonnage shipped through the Port of Sacramento. From a 1981 high of 3.3 million tons, port cargoes plummeted to below one million tons in 1987.

Nonetheless, port director John Sulpizle says the port's best days lie ahead. In 1988, port throughput exceeded 1.3 million tons, and Sulpizle is forecasting a steady 3 to 4 percent annual increase. "We were really hurt by the adjustment in the 1980s, no question," says Sulpizle. "But we think our new

foreign trade zone and deepening the channel again will begin turning things around for the port."

The $76-million channel deepening was begun in early 1990 and will be completed in seven years. Where the 30-foot-deep port can now receive only 20 percent of all ocean-going vessels trading in the Pacific Rim, the new 35-foot channel will allow it to receive 75 percent of the Rim's fleet, therby making it an attractive alternative to more expensive San Francisco Bay area ports. Sacramento's status as a highway transportation hub is also expected to attract clients intent on transhipping goods. In addition, the port is instituting a container ferry service where barges will piggyback container cars running from Sacramento to Bay Area ports and back again.

The foreign trade zone should bring more immediate revenue to the port. Warehouse construction began in January 1990 and was completed in January 1991.

Located on an 8.3-acre site adjacent to the port's front gate, the foreign trade zone will provide the port with a duty deferral area to allow shippers the opportunity of re-exporting and manufacturing as a way of avoiding costly levies. According to Sulpizle, the intent is twofold: "The foreign trade zone invites commerce by allowing clients to increase their cash-flow and it also creates jobs for the local economy."

Military and Aerospace
Though Sacramento has had a military presence almost since its founding, it wasn't until the First World War that the military became a powerful force in the local economy.

Mather Field, located in what is now the suburb of Rancho Cordova, was the first local outpost of note when the army air corps established it as a pilot training

school in 1918.

Then, in 1942, the army established a Signal Corps Depot on the site of the old state fairgrounds at the corner of Stockton Boulevard and Broadway, moving in 1945 to its present location on Fruitridge Road in eastern Sacramento County.

The newly created air force was the next to arrive, in 1948. The air force took over a 3,800-acre site on Watt Avenue, assuming control of it from the army. Previously known as the Sacramento Air Material Area, the base was renamed McClellan Air Force Base in 1948.

Throughout the Second World War and up to the present, the military has assumed an ever-increasing role in the local economy, employing nearly 28,000 (mostly civilian) workers with annual budgets in excess of $3.7 billion and payrolls of nearly $1 billion. McClellan, the largest military installation in the Sacramento area, alone employs 17,000 workers with an annual budget of $3.4 billion and a payroll of $545 million.

As goes America's involvement in foreign wars, so have gone local military's employment rolls and budgets. During the height of the Vietnam War, McClellan employed more than 26,000 workers. But as the economy settled into a peace-time mode, the military presence decreased, and in the case of Mather Field, dried up all together. Mather, once the main training base for B-52 navigators, was recently ordered closed by the Defense Department in a budget-cutting move. Though still in operation, Mather will officially close in 1993. Beale Air Force Base, in nearby Marysville, will assume Mather's navigational training function.

Aerojet-General: Rocket Plant at Prairie City
In the 1950s and 1960s a war of a different sort—a Cold War—saw a new military-oriented employer move to the Sacramento area. These newly arrived warriors were of a decidedly different stripe. Instead of brass and braid, they wore lab coats and carried clipboards. Generals, colonels, and majors took a back seat to clinicians, chemists, and engineers when Aerojet-General Corporation arrived in Sacramento in 1951.

Aerojet had left its parent plant in Azusa, California, when the expansion of Los Angeles threatened it with sub-urban encroachment. Aerojet built rockets and motors, not

exactly the kind of industry compatible with single-family homes and shopping centers. They needed room to grow and began searching for a new site. In Sacramento, they found what they were seeking.

Along Highway 50 near the town of Folsom, there was an old Gold Rush town called Prairie City, once the home of 3,500 prospectors. By the 1860s, Prairie City had dried up. Subsequent hydraulic mining pretty well chewed up the area, and when Aerojet acquired the 13,300-acre site all that remained of the gold industry were a few shacks, placer tailings, and hillocks formed by upturned earth. It looked like a moonscape, which dovetailed presisely with what Aerojet would soon have in mind.

In the early 1950s Aerojet used the site to build Titan I and Titan II ICBM missiles. Eventually they would build more than 1,000 missiles in the Titan series. The purpose of this production was closing the Cold War "missile gap."

But when the Soviet Union launched the Sputnik satellite in 1957, Aerojet widened its focus and turned to the "space race." Now Aerojet's charge was twofold: build ICBM rockets and motors and also build rockets and motors to put a man on the moon.

In 1953, Aerojet employed 771 workers. By 1963, that number had grown to nearly 20,000 workers on three different shifts occupying 800 separate buildings and 30 different rocket lines.

The Vietnam War caused the federal government to divert resources from the space race to a grittier reality. With it, Aerojet employment fell through the floor, plumeting to a low of 1,500 by the mid-1970s.

Now Aerojet is again back on the rise. With the growing

international market for commercial satellites, Aerojet has been transforming Titan ICBMs into peacetime-purpose rockets—"beating our swords into plowshares" is how Aerojet spokesman Tom Fitzgerald describes it. Currently employing 3,900 workers with an annual payroll of $175 million and a budget of more than $500 million, Aerojet is the largest private employer in Sacramento County.

The advent of *glasnost* and *perestroika* caused Aerojet to diversify even further. Now Aerojet chemists are involved in mass-producing designer chemicals for AIDS and cancer treatment. However, Aerojet is still maintaining its lead in rocketry. Aerojet has the contract for the "head eye" construction for the High-Indo-Atmospheric Defense Interceptor in the Star Wars program and is also working with Lockheed on designing the improved solid rocket boosters for the space shuttle.

Lately, Aerojet has been teaming up with another defense contractor, the McDonnell-Douglas Corporation, to build components for the National Aero-Space Plane, or NASP.

The NASP is a space plane capable of taking off from conventional airports and carrying payloads into space at speeds of more than 5,000 miles per hour. Though intended as a NASA space vehicle, the NASP has also been dis-

cussed as a commercial jetliner that will make the Concorde a comaparative slow boat to China. "A coast-to-coast run would take about an hour," says Fitzgerald, "and a trip to Tokyo would take three."

Silicon Valley East: The Arrival of High Tech

Prior to 1970, Sacramento's share of jobs in the high-technology fields of computers, electronics, and technical instruments manufacturing was so miniscule it was hardly worth mentioning. In 1970, only 600 Sacramentans held jobs in the high-tech industry, only .04 percent of all high-tech jobs nationally.

But by the mid-1970s the local high-tech market began slowly to improve. By the end of the decade, Sacramento had doubled its national share of the high-tech market. Still, at only 1,700 employees, Sacramento could hardly hold a candle to the mecca of high tech, Santa Clara County's Silicon Valley.

As was the case with Aerojet, overcrowding in the Silicon Valley and the upward-spiraling price of land caused high-tech manufacturers to begin seeking wider, and greener, pastures. And like the placer miners of the previous century, where most of those high-tech prospectors headed was to the foothills outside Sacramento. INTEL chose the city of Folsom. NEC, the Japanese electronics manufacturer, chose Roseville. And so did the grandaddy of domestic high-tech manufacturers, Hewlett-Packard.

In 1984, the number of high-tech jobs in the Sacramento area had increased to nearly 2,800. Between 1984 and the end of the decade, the number rose dramatically, to 14,000 by 1989. But some projections show that by the end of the century the Sacramento area could have as many as 120,000 high-tech workers.

Aerojet may hold the current distinction as the area's largest private employer, but that will shortly change. Like Aerojet, the company that will supplant it was born in the World War II era when two Stanford electrical engineering graduates set up an electronics lab in a rented garage. The company they formed was called Hewlett-Packard.

Above: Herman Miller's architecturally stunning Rocklin complex, located in Stanford Ranch, manufactures office systems and furniture and is expected to employ 400 workers by 1992. Photo by Bob Rowan/Progressive Image Photography

Facing page: The South Natomas office parks attest to the fact that Sacramento suburbs are now thriving commercial centers in their own right. Photo by Tom Myers

Headquartered in Cupertino, Hewlett-Packard expanded to the Sacramento area in 1979, choosing a 500-acre site on the outskirts of Roseville. The rural setting, with its three low-rise buildings of 1.5 million square feet, five-acre recreation center, 5,000-square-foot pavillion, field house, and two baseball diamonds, seems more like a college campus than it does a high-tech manufacturing center, which was by intent, says Hewlett-Packard's Ken Larson. "The atmosphere we like to maintain is very informal," he says. "People dress casually and everybody is on a first-name basis."

The casualness Larson speaks of is more present in the upstairs management section of the H-P plant than it is on the downstairs manufacturing floor. The dress code may still be laid-back here, but the pace isn't. "We have a system here where if we get a rush order from Timbuktu and a major customer just lost their system, we can go to our computer and pull our client's card and find out if that system is in stock. We can also find out if one is in the manufacturing process," says Larson. "If it isn't we can turn around a finished product in 17 hours, and that's on over 300 different products."

By the end of the century, Hewlett-Packard will occupy 5 million square feet and have 20,000 employees. Directly across Blue Ravine Road from Hewlett-Packard is NEC's Roseville semiconductor plant which employs 700 workers, a number expected to double by the end of the century. The two main high-tech firms in Folsom, semiconductor manufacturer INTEL and Avantek, Inc, which manufactures microwave components, will also double their current com-

bined employment of 1,500. The same projections hold true across the board for other Sacramento-based high-tech firms like Cable-Data and Systems Integrators, Inc.

3M, the Minnesota-based manufacturer, has also chosen a Roseville site as its future west coast headquarters. The 140-acre 3M site at the intersection of Interstate 80 and Douglas Boulevard is expected to employ 5,000 workers by the end of the century.

SACTO: Catalysts of Commerce

Much of the credit for Sacramento's high-tech industry gains can be claimed by the Sacramento Area Commerce and Trade Organization (SACTO), the local nonprofit development organization established in 1975.

The brainchild of Sacramento media magnate John Kelly, SACTO formulated a plan of action to attract the best of the world's corporations to Sacramento.

As former SACTO president John Roberts describes it, the plan was simple. "We researched who we wanted to attract here by poring over books like *The 100 Best Companies in America, Fortune* magazine's list of the 100 most-admired companies in America, and the Tom Peters management series. We wanted good-neighbor-type companies and we decided to do what we could to attract those companies to come here. Every year for the past five years, we've been able to attract one of those companies."

And with each new arrival, other admired companies began looking to Sacramento as a site of possible expansion. Companies like furniture manufacturer Herman Miller, 3M, The Dana Corporation, and H.B. Fuller and Company. As Roberts says, "We found that quality companies beget quality companies, and that quality companies want to locate in quality communities. This was really how we sold them on Sacramento."

Currently, SACTO has 380 members in the four-county metropolitan Sacramento area (Yolo, Placer, El Dorado, and Sacramento) and their aggressvie policy of combing the world in search of its best and brightest corporations has made these companies stand up and take notice of Sacramento.

Herman Miller: The Futurists of Stanford Ranch

On a rolling hillside between Roseville and the town of Rocklin is an industrial business park called Stanford Ranch. There you'll find a complex of buildings that arrests the

attention of passersby. The complex is the home of the Herman Miller Company, a Michigan-based furniture manufacturer.

You would have to be asleep not to notice the plant.

Herman Miller's Rocklin complex is probably the most architecturally distinctive structure in the entire Sacramento area. Clad in a galvanized steel skin with exposed rivets, the complexes' two warehouse-sized buildings form the arms of a "Y" that meet in an open area covered by a copper-plated, post-and-girder tower. Next to the tower, a neo-classical audio visual center and showroom creates a marriage of two divergent styles which somehow works.

Designed by Los Angeles architect Frank Gehry, the 600,000-square-foot plant was first opened for warehousing and transshipping goods in early 1989, but has recently begun manufacturing. When it is completely built out and

occupied by 1992, the Herman Miller facility will employ 400 workers.

The company that pioneered the idea of office systems products and designed the ergonomic chair chose the Stanford Ranch site as its manufacturing and distribution center for the entire west coast. A recognized industry leader for its innovative approach in all aspects of operation—from the architecture it chooses for its plants, to its employee participation in management and ownership, to the twenty-first-century products it builds—Herman Miller came to Sacramento in 1988, attracted by what plant general manager Chris Dancy calls "Sacramento's sense of purpose."

"Many things attracted us to Sacramento but in a nutshell it was this: We look for an area that fits in with our corporate philosophy, communities with a sense of purpose where our employees can say 'I belong there.'" Dancy says

Above: Affordable homes in traditional suburban settings are one reason why people choose the Sacramento area as a place to live. Photo by Tom Myers

Facing page: Attractive new residences like this one in El Dorado Hills are being developed in planned communities designed to meet the needs of Sacramento's growing population. Photo by Tom Myers

they found that here in the Sacramento area. "This is an area that's balanced. People here aren't pro growth or no growth; they're *controlled* growth. It's sophisticated but casual. It has a sense of purpose and stays focused on it."

Construction: Boom Industry

Between 1940 and 1959 the population of metropolitan Sacramento more than tripled—from 150,000 to more than 500,000. In the next 30 years it nearly tripled again to its current population of just under 1.5 million. The city added new suburbs in the north, south, and east, and absorbed older townships like Florin, Fair Oaks, and Orangevale. What this massive expansion of metropolitan Sacramento has meant for the local construction industry is measured in the jobs and opportunities it has created. Currently more than 24,000 Sacramentans are employed in construction

trades and the industry accounts for revenues totaling $2.5 billion a year. And with more new arrivals making their way to Sacramento—a steady 4 percent population increase that translates to 50,000 new residents a year—the future construction market is projected to show steady gains throughout the rest of the century.

Commercial, retail, road, residential, and industrial construction have grown steadily in Sacramento for the past half-century. But the megaboom that began in the 1980s propelled the construction economy like an Aerojet rocket booster. Jobs increased by 25 percent, salaries by more than 50 percent. Between 1986 and 1988 alone, 90 new shopping centers increased retail space by 16 percent to 29 million square feet. The industrial market grew steadily as well, if a bit more slowly, at 13 percent per year. But the office market accelerated into the ionosphere. Between 1984 and 1988, commercial office construction increased 144 percent and became a $1 billion a year industry.

"Back in the 1960s, I couldn't have anticipated the commercial growth that we're seeing now," says Marvin T. "Buzz" Oates, who began developing warehouses in Sacramento in the 1950s. Oates, one of Sacramento's most visible developers, has been at it longer than anyone in the area and says that the current trend will continue throughout the rest of the century. "We might not grow at the fantastic rate we've grown at in the 1980s, but commercial development will remain a strong component of this economy. Why? Because Sacramento has attractions you can't find in bigger cities like the Bay Area and Los Angeles. Our location is prime, the cost of land is low, and the quality of life here is good. And it's not just the city of Sacramento, but the whole Sacramento Valley."

Though the downtown office market has been the most visible center of commercial concentration, office construction is hardly relegated to the grid as new commercial centers like North and South Natomas, the Century City-like Point West office complexes, and new office buildings along Highway 50 and in Roseville and Folsom attest.

Thirty years before, Sacramento had been an aging metropolitan center surrounded by a handful of suburbs, but now those suburbs have commercial centers of their own.

As these areas grew commercially, metropolitan Sacramento expanded even further. New residential clustering began occurring in Folsom, Roseville, Elk Grove, and other towns that Sacramentans used to think of as "out in the country." Thousands of acres of what were once farms of played-out gold diggings were rezoned for new residential development. From a post-recession 1980 low of 6,700 new housing units totaling less than $250 million in value, by 1989 local residential contractors built more than 18,000 new units totaling more than $1 billion in value.

The mushrooming metropolis of the 1980s presented a problem. The bargain that turned Sacramento from a best-kept secret to an eighties boom town is in some ways a double-edged sword: as Sacramento mushroomed, traffic congestion increased and air quality declined. What draws new companies and new residents to Sacramento is its quality of life. The challenge Sacramento faces is in maintaining that quality of life while simultaneously accommodating its vast metropolitan expansion.

Anyone who could pull the sword from that stone would need the aid of a magician. Developer Phil Angelides had just such a Merlin in mind: a U.C. Berkeley urban design professor by the name of Peter Calthorpe.

Calthorpe was no stranger to Sacramento. He'd lived here when serving in the Jerry Brown administration as assistant to state architect Sim Van der Ryn and had requited himself capably during that tenure, personally overseeing construction on the solar-energy-efficient Bateson Building that houses the state resources department and then building a low-cost downtown housing project called Somerset Parkside.

After leaving the Brown administration, Calthorpe began evolving a development model called "pedestrian pockets," a more energy-efficient, mixed-use suburb in which all houses would be clustered within walking distance of a town center where commercial development would be concentrated along a light rail stop. Calthorpe knew it worked theoretically—if you provided jobs and services in a suburb, you eliminated the need for commuting. And if you had light rail within a quarter-mile radius of where you lived, 4 out of 10 times you would use it when you had to commute. The net effect would be a self-contained mini-city in the suburbs that penciled out to a 70 percent reduction in smog-producing automobile travel.

Angelides, a young developer and power in local Democratic party circles, went for the idea. He hired Calthorpe to redesign a 1,000-acre tract in his Laguna Creek development by Elk Grove and reconfigured it as the first pedestrian pocket development to be built in the United States.

Begun in the summer of 1990, the Laguna pocket will accommodate 2,000 new residents in a community whose town center is located along a man-made lake. "This plan reflects the best of this new concept, along with those features which historically have made Sacramento a great place to live," says Angelides. "I know we're going a bit out on a limb with this because it's never been tried. But if we succeed, you're going to see a lot of this development."

Angelides' prophecy isn't just wishful thinking. Sacramento County's new general plan is expected to call for at least 30 percent of all new suburban development to be pedestrian pocket oriented, and Gregg Lukenbill is also developing part of his North Natomas tract as a pedestrian pocket. "This is an idea whose time has come," says Lukenbill, "and I think you'll find that the market is ready to support it."

Government:
A Recession-Proof Economy

When Sacramentans go to work, 3 out of every 10 go to work at a government job: 170,000 work for the state, federal, or local governments, and it is from this powerful force that Sacramento derives its reputation as a "recession-proof economy." State government provides 100,000 jobs; local government employs another 35,000 workers; and federal workers total almost 30,000.

The Building—the state capitol—is the center of Sacramento's state government activity, and the agency buildings which surround it form the second tier. What was once a relatively small part of Sacramento's economy in its early years is now its most powerful component.

The government is conspicuous downtown, but it is ubiquitous throughout Sacramento. Midtown, the south area, the north area, and the Highway 50 corridor all house government employment centers of one sort or another.

Though government jobs increased in number during the 1980s, they began showing an actual decline in the percentage share they once had in Sacramento. Now the growth industries are construction, manufacturing, services, finance, and real estate.

Which is a good thing for Sacramento as far as Assemblyman Phil Isenberg is concerned. Isenberg, Sacramento's mayor from 1975 through 1983, sees the dropoff in government employment as "a sign that there's more here than just state jobs, which was how people once tended to perceive Sacramento. Now it's high tech, manufacturing, service industries, you name it. I think the kind of transformation we've seen here just in the economy in the past 20 years is extraordinary. I guess you could say that we're a city that has arrived."

Above: Tourism is an integral part of Sacramento's economy and visitors to the area have a number of fine bed-and-breakfast establishments to choose from. Photo by Ed Asmus

Facing page, top: Retail centers in the Sacramento area suburbs are thriving. Seen here is Natoma Station, a bustling mall in Folsom. Photo by Tom Myers

Facing page, bottom: Government continues to be Sacramento's steadiest employer, with three out of every 10 residents working for local, state, or federal agencies. Photo by Bob Rowan/Progressive Image Photography

Halls of Learning, Havens for Healing

E | **ducation: An Overview**

Dr. Robert Jones sits at his desk in the administration building of California State University Sacramento and muses to a visiting reporter. "One day I'd like to see someone do a survey on the total education expenditures in the Sacramento area. It's my guess that this area has the richest outlay per capita of any city in California." The vice president for university affairs should have bet that hunch, for the nearly $3.5 billion in total education budgets allocated yearly in metropolitan Sacramento works out to a per capita figure of almost $10,000 per student, a figure that is indeed the state's highest.

From business and trade schools, to community colleges, to its two major universities, Sacramento's educational spectrum offers a broad variety of academic and career disciplines at a score of urban and suburban campuses located within the 50-mile radius of the four-county metropolitan area.

Business and professional training came first to the valley, in the late nineteenth century, and continues still at new business training centers like National College, MTI, and the Heald Business College.

Higher education arrived later, and Sacramento's first few postsecondary institutions often had to share classroom space with the local high schools from which they sprang. Such was the case with Sacramento City College, originally housed at Sacramento High School, and the first incarnation of Sierra College (nee Placer College) when they bused in students from foothill towns to the old Placer High School campus in Auburn.

It's a far cry from what Sacramento's higher education is today, with downtown campuses like the USC Postgraduate School of Public Administration and the University of Pacific-affiliated McGeorge Law School offering postgraduate programs while mega-universities like CSUS and UC Davis strain to keep pace with increased enrollments, and the four

Computer literacy begins early for Sacramento's elementary school students. Photo by Tom Myers

community colleges operate at full capacity day and night.

Sacramento's now-fertile environment for higher education blossomed in less than a century, germinated from the seed of an idea planted in the mind of one Peter J. Shields when he was secretary of the annual Agricultural Society Exhibition, an event later known as the California State Fair.

UC Davis

The seed took root during a discussion about butter.

On a hot summer day in 1898, a man named Robert Saylor entered Shields' office to announce that Humboldt County had just won the butter competition gold ribbon. "How do you judge butter?" Shields asked. Saylor, the dairy department chief, explained the subtleties for him. Shields asked Saylor where he'd learned this, and Saylor replied that he'd studied at Penn State's agricultural school. Shields concluded that a farm state like California ought to have such a school, and over the next decade made it his mission to establish one.

Sheilds' concept for an agricultural college was supported by the California Creamery Operators Association and the state Livestock Breeders Association. But the idea didn't sit too well with the powerful interests who controlled higher ed-

ucation at the time, the University of California at Berkeley and the Board of Regents they essentially controlled. When Shields made his case to one regent, he was summarily dismissed: "*That* thing," sniffed the regent, "is not education."

After two failed attempts, in 1905 the state legislature finally approved Shields' plan for an experimental agricultural farm that would be an off-campus affiliate of UC Berkeley.

Seven hundred and seventy-nine acres on three separate tracts of land were purchased near the small town of Davis, 15 miles west of Sacramento. In 1908, construction began on two cottages, a dairy building, and an octagonal stock-judging building. That fall, a short program in agricultural sciences was convened. Practical instruction began the following January. In April, the public was invited to come out and view the new experimental farm. They eagerly obliged, arriving by train from Sacramento, Stockton, Berkeley, and San Francisco with picnic baskets in tow, a yearly ritual repeated every April now known as Davis Picnic Day.

Across the lagoon from the sixth floor of Mrak Hall, the administration building of the University of California at Davis, you can still see the Octagon Building. But not much else of the original agriculture farm resembles the present university which has since grown to 3,600 acres, 1,600 faculty members, and 23,000 students. It is the largest in size, second-largest in budget, and third-largest in enrollment of

the nine campuses which constitute the University of California system.

Gaining its autonomy from Berkeley in 1952, Davis grew from the original college of agriculture to include two other colleges: engineering, and arts & sciences. These three colleges encompass seven separate schools of the sprawling campus on Putah Creek, including a veterinary school which is the number one school of its kind in the country, a medical school, a law school, and the most recent addition, a graduate school of management.

Sampling the Specializations at UC Davis

Once known for its agricultural specialization, UC Davis now offers a comprehensive blend of all academic fields. Though the agriculture school which inspired its founding continues to be recognized as one of the world's finest, the art & letters school has gained considerable esteem since the mid-1960s.

Perhaps the most esteemed is Davis's fine arts department, whose faculty has included internationally acclaimed artists like Wayne Thiebaud, Manuel Neri, William T. Wiley, and Robert Arneson.

The Thiebaud/Arneson group helped establish Davis as one of the top-flight university art departments in America, and the effect they had on the so-called "West Coast

Above: Heald Business College is one of several fine business training centers in Sacramento. Photo by Richard Kaylin

Facing page, top: The McGeorge School of Law is renowned for its courtroom with built-in videotaping equipment that enables aspiring lawyers and their professors to review proceedings. Photo by Tom Myers

Facing page, bottom: Founded in 1971, National University is a private, nonprofit institution offering higher education opportunities to career-oriented adults. Photo by Richard Kaylin

School" helped alter the once-common perception that Davis was *just* an "Aggie" school.

So did the establishment of the Martin Luther King Law School when it opened in 1968. Once known more for the controversial Bakke case that challenged affirmative action admissions, in the past few years Davis's law program has been noted more for the quality of its instruction. Ranked as one of the top 25 law schools in the country, 88 percent of Davis's 1989 King graduates passed the bar examinations on their first try, ranking them third in the state in this category. (McGeorge holds the number one ranking.) That same year, Davis's law students further distinguished themselves by winning the National Moot

Above: The programs offered by Sacramento City College are varied, ranging from aeronautics to nursing to cosmetology. Photo by Richard Kaylin

Left: The campus of UC Davis is the largest in the UC system, sprawling across 3,600 acres. Here students make their way across the landscaped grounds. Photo by Tom Myers

Court competition, the first west coast school to achieve the honor.

An intimate school of 500 with its own on-site library, MLK is a campus within a campus which maintains the excellence of its instruction through a near one-to-one faculty-student ratio.

On the other side of the campus, pure science takes precedence over arts and the law. Here, UCD med school students receive their undergraduate training. Here, too, is where one of only seven national "Centers for AIDS Research" is located.

Its university research facilities and Med Center hospital in nearby Sacramento made Davis a natural choice for an AIDS research center. What sealed it, though, was UC Davis's primate center. This would allow clinicians to test advances in AIDS research and treatment on an animal that AIDS Research Center director Dr. Murray F. Gardner calls "the gold standard."

Working primarily with rhesus monkeys, Gardner and his staff believe the progress they've made wouldn't have been possible without the primate center, and that a first-stage vaccine for AIDS is as soon as two years away.

Like its sister school across the Yolo causeway, the birth of Sacramento's in-town university was a long-term pregnancy attended by the same reluctant midwives.

In the middle of the 1930s, as Sacramento entered one of its periodic growth spurts, a number of city fathers began voicing their opinion that California's capital city deserved its own four-year university to prepare local students for professional life. Again, UC Berkeley and the powerful lobbying forces they brought to bear on the Board of Regents opposed the idea.

In this case, Sacramento's chamber of commerce served the same essential function as the breeders and growers associations did in the founding of UC Davis.

It took ten years and seven separate tries for chamber of commerce member Lester R. Daniels and his legislative cohort, local state senator Earl R. Desmond, to secure passage of the bill that created what would become California State University, Sacramento.

Originally housed on the same campus as Sacramento City College, CSUS left its temporary quarters in 1953 and moved to a 288-acre site in East Sacramento in what used

"When you have a primate like the rhesus whose simian AIDS virus is very similar to human AIDS, you have a model that gives you a clear understanding of the pathogenesis of this retro virus," Gardner says. "There's a tremendous sense of urgency to what we're doing, but we have a very unique resource here and we're eager to show results."

Just west of the main campus cluster is where Davis's premier veterinary school is housed. Established in 1946, the school of veterinary science initially specialized in large animal medicine but has since shifted its emphasis to smaller pet animals as well.

"The thing that gives this school the claim to being number one is the vast amount of research that occurs here, which is part of the mandate we have as a university," says associate dean Dr. Don Low. Active in the AIDS research program, the veterinary school also includes an equine research center where many of the country's top thoroughbred racehorses are treated.

UCD's founding father is commemorated by the 2.1 million-volume library named in his honor, and Shields' spirit can rest easy with Davis's advancement of its original agricultural purpose. In a self-published memoir, Shields wrote, "The farmer's life is mostly emulative, rather than competitive. He can rejoice in his neighbor's success without fearing it will impair his own."

The experimental agricultural farm may now be a megacampus, but the entrepreneurial agrarian spirit which Peter Shields fought to instill it with still infuses the university and continues to play a significant role in its future.

to be a peach orchard bordered by hop fields and goat farms.

Between 1965 and 1971 the enrollment at CSUS skyrocketed from 6,000 to 15,000, and its budget tripled from $7.7 million to more than $23 million. By the end of that era, the campus was almost entirely built out. And yet the enrollment showed no signs of leveling off.

With its limited space, CSUS, like the city itself, grew up rather than out. Currently in the midst of a master plan expansion that will see $214 million in new construction take place over the next 20 years, the campus originally built for a maximum enrollment of 6,000 now has more than 25,000 students and plans to accommodate another 5,000 at future off-campus sites and through telecommuting and year-round, state-funded summer sessions. The master plan will not only increase CSUS's capacity but change its look and feel from a two-story business park-like environment to a futuristic-looking campus predominated by high-rise buildings.

The master construction plan currently underway that will continue until 2010 has already produced a state-of-the-art computer science building and a new library extension and will soon result in new classroom buildings, additional science & engineering and music buildings, and a University Union annex.

Above: Students at CSU Sacramento find that bikes are a great way to get around. Photo by Bob Rowan/ Progressive Image Photography

Facing page, top: Decorative murals brighten up many of the buildings on the CSU Sacramento campus. Photo by Tom Myers

Facing page, bottom: Fine arts students at UC Davis benefit from instruction by a faculty composed of professional artists such as Mick Sheldon, seen here with his work. Photo by Richard Kaylin

CSUS Centers of Excellence

Sixteen hundred CSUS faculty members provide instruction at the East Sacramento campus and the 13-county area CSUS serves is second in size only to that of CSU Chico. The excellence of many of CSUS's departments—especially its education and business schools and its criminal justice and government programs—attracts growing numbers of students from well outside the Sacramento area.

The CSUS school of business is the number one business school in Northern California, as is the school of education, which confers nearly 50 percent of all the teaching credentials granted by the five state universities in Northern California.

***Above:** The new library at CSU Sacramento is part of the current master construction plan that is to continue until 2010. The library is but one of the ultramodern buildings that will transform the face of the campus. Photo by Tom Myers*

***Facing page, top:** CSU Sacramento occupies a 288-acre campus on the banks of the American River. Here students traverse Guy West Bridge, which links the campus to University Avenue. Photo by Bob Rowan/Progressive Image Photography*

***Facing page, bottom:** Established in 1916, Sacramento Community College is part of an extensive system of two-year schools offering students job skills and a springboard to further education. Photo by Bob Rowan/Progressive Image Photography*

One of the fastest-growing departments at CSUS has been the computer sciences and engineering program, which just moved in to a new $13-million, 55,000-square-foot building. The building itself is a living experiment of germane interest to Northern Californians.

Fitted with 290 strain gauges incorporated into its structure and wired to a central computer, the computer science and engineering center was designed as a "live" building to monitor the effects of earthquakes and give an immediate assessment of their effects on structural integrity.

Like UC Davis, CSUS takes great pride in its fine arts program, which has helped encourage the development of local artists and has employed a number of distinguished faculty members like Gladys Neilsen, Jim Nutt, William Allen, Joan Moment, and founding faculty member Robert Else.

With its proximity to the state capitol it's not surprising that CSUS's government studies program attracts students intent on pursuing careers in politics. The recently added Center for California Studies extends CSUS's leadership in this field by providing grants and internships to both students and visiting fellows.

More than an academic center, the university also plays a leading role in shaping community issues and has sponsored conferences on regional growth and other topics of concern to the future of the Sacramento metropolitan area. Robert Jones, CSUS vice-president for university affairs, explains the reasoning behind this: "We're seeking some continuity of purpose in this university's relationship to the community, and we're trying to be a major player in helping shape this community's future."

Community Colleges

Besides the two major universities, metropolitan Sacramento also has four community colleges where more than 75,000

students can complete undergraduate classes preparatory to transferring to a four-year institution, complete programs toward an associate of arts (AA) degree, or receive advanced or preliminary job training.

Part undergraduate studies, part adult education centers, part vocational training center, the community colleges offer Sacramento students a variety of specialized academic career programs that dovetail with the needs of local industries.

Albert Rodda, one of Sacramento's most fervent believers and supporters of the community college system, sees the two-year institutions as "the ladder to upward mobility that penetrates the deepest and offers the most opportunity to the greatest amount of the population." A native

Sacramentan and the former chairman of the senate education committee, Senator Rodda now serves on the Los Rios Community College Board. "We tend to overlook the value the community colleges have to our society," he says. "They're a vastly underrated resource."

Whether it's Sacramento City College's aeronautics, nursing, and cosmetology programs or American River College's emphasis on computer science and technology, Sierra College's suburban agriculture and railroad equipment management programs, or the administration of justice program at Cosumnes College that many of Sacramento's finest participate in prior to entering the police academies, the local community colleges provide an important two-way bridge between students and career choices indigenous to the region.

Hospitals

From its earliest recorded history when its first hospitals were built to aid the victims of the cholera epidemic of 1850, Sacramento has provided comprehensive health care service to the entire Central Valley.

With one exception, those first few hospitals, including one located at Sutter's Fort itself, are remembered only in the yellowed annals which acknowledge their existence. The one exception is what was once called the Sacramento County Home, an institution now known as the University of California Medical Center, or more easily by its nickname, the Med Center.

UCD Med Center: Headquarters of "Hospital Row"

"I guess you could say that what's being created along here is something of a Hospital Row," says Dr. Frank Loge, chief hospital administrator of the UCD Medical Center.

The Med Center complex, a warren of the old, the new, and the in-between, strings out along Stockton Boulevard from the old state fairgrounds at the corner of Broadway to Alhambra Boulevard two miles north. Its clinics, department headquarters, and doctors' offices line the west side of Stockton

while the main hospital tower and the administration buildings occupy the east side of the street.

For 120 years there has been a hospital at the Oak Knoll site on what used to be called the Lower Stockton Road. The Med Center continues one of the primary objectives of its antecedent—the care of the county's indigent. But since 1973, when the university assumed control of the hospital from the county, the Med Center has expanded that function and now provides a much wider range of services to the community—from emergency and trauma treatment centers that are the valley's largest, to oncology and intensive care, to the latest technological advances in *in vitro* fertiliza-

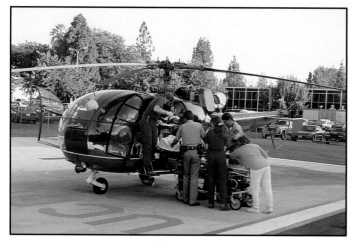

tion and skin-farming for treating burn victims, to becoming the first hospital in Northern California to successfully perform a rarely attempted pancreatic transplant.

"We receive a good deal of recognition for our emergency treatment and trauma center," says UCDMC spokesperson Susan Maderious-Mayer. "But the teaching part of our mission is not very well understood or appreciated, and we need to better communicate this aspect of the hospital. We teach students, train residents, and train fellows here—people at all levels of medical training. And it really has great value to this community because the doctor in Roseville or Fair Oaks or Carmichael who's your family doctor was probably trained right here at UCD."

With a medical staff of more than 700 and a hospital staff approaching 4,000, the 470-bed Med Center facility is now in the process of consolidating its sprawl through an extensive 20-year, $580-million expansion program that will nearly double its capacity and concentrate hospital functions into specific zones.

Two more hospital towers will soon be added to the single

one which presently exists. Two new administrative buildings, a psychiatric wing, a teaching/nursing home, a rehabilitation center, and a faculty club and conference center are also part of the master plan. Most of the expansion is currently underway, and nearly half the total budget will be expended between 1989 and 1995. "This is a very exciting time for us," says Maderious-Mayer. "We just can't build buildings fast enough to keep up with our growth and the patient demand."

One demand in particular is for additional bed space for the hospital's Burn Center.

The UCDMC Burn Center has just 12 beds to serve a 25-county area that's roughly the size of the state of Illinois. But even so, the tiny unit is one of the first in the country to advance a burn treatment technique called a "cultured autograph."

B.J. Berensen, head nurse of the Burn Center, explains the process. "One of the most devastating aspects of being seriously burned is the psychological trauma that the patient has to endure because of the scarring that results from skin-grafting. Well, in a cultured autograph, a small portion of the patient's own skin is removed and grown through genetic inducement—skin-farming, if you will. The best thing about it is that it doesn't have the scarring effect that typical grafting entails."

The advances made in burn treatment technology are mirrored by others occurring elsewhere at the sprawling Med Center, says Maderious-Mayer. "We're making breakthroughs in AIDS research and treatment, cancer research and treatment, in cardiac surgery, the pancreatic transplant, or almost any other major disease entity. This is a very exciting time for us. There's something new that's happening here every day."

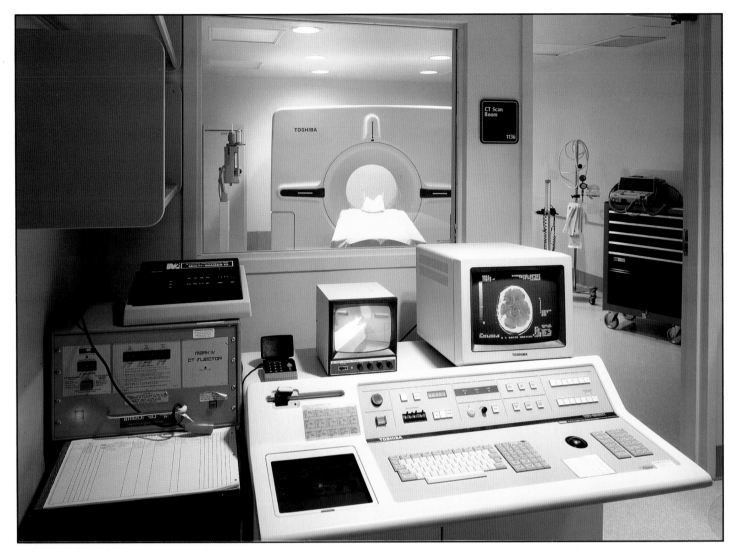

The Sutter System

For much of Northern California—from Sacramento to the Oregon line and even beyond—the name Sutter has become near synonymous with major health care needs. Sutter provides its patients with a comprehensive health care umbrella spanning the breadth of Northern California where the latest technological advances pioneered at its two major Sacramento hospitals are readily available to its smaller regional hospitals in Brookings, Oregon, Crescent City, Vallejo, and Davis, and the three other hopsitals and four local nursing centers that comprise the Sutter Health System.

Like the founder of the city where it was born and from whom it derived its name, a pioneering spirit has characterized Sutter hospitals since the first one opened its doors in 1923.

The system began with the founding of Sutter General Hospital. Located directly opposite Sutter's Fort, Sutter General was the first air conditioned hospital in the state and at one time possessed the most powerful cancer radiation unit in all of California. That original structure, removed in 1988 and replaced with a new 400-bed facility and adjoining administrative wing, is now the orthopedic, neuroscience, and diabetes treatment center, while Sutter Memorial, its younger offshoot in East Sacramento, is most renowned for its excellence in cardiac surgery, oncology, perontology, and as *the* birthing center of Northern California.

"People are always confusing the two—Sutter General and Sutter Memorial," says Sutter Memorial spokeswoman Beatrix Wilson. "We like to think of ourselves as one big hospital with specialties divided between two locations. But the easiest way to remember the distinction is that we're the baby hospital."

Which is how Sutter Memorial began—as Sutter Maternity Hospital, in 1937.

The facility at 52nd and F streets had 52 maternity beds when it first opened. Two hundred thousand babies later, Sutter Memorial is now a 375-bed facility. Six thousand babies a year are born at Memorial. The hospital is the center for all of Northern California's high-risk pregnancies and is where chronically ill newborn infants within the region are transferred.

One of the more revolutionary techniques developed at Sutter Memorial is called Extra Corporeal Membrane Oxygen-

Above: UC Davis Medical Center's facilities include state-of-the-art equipment for diagnosis and treatment, such as this CAT scan room. Photo by Cathy Kelly Architectural Photography, courtesy, John F. Otto Inc.

Facing page, top: Inland Northern California's only academic hospital, UC Davis Medical Center is committed to training the medical professionals of tomorrow. Photo by Cathy Kelly Architectural Photography, courtesy, John F. Otto Inc.

Facing page, bottom: The UC Davis Medical Center's Life Flight, an emergency transport helicopter, provides speedy access for the region's critically ill and injured patients. Photo by Tom Myers

ation. ECMO treats term infants born with chronic respiratory defects by circulating the blood outside the body. "The success rate we've had with ECMO has been excellent," says Wilson. "We've been doing this for about two and a half years and have performed maybe 60 procedures, without which the survival rate is only 20 percent."

Memorial was also the first hospital in Northern California with a complete heart transplant program. Launched in 1988, the cardiac center performs more than 1,000 transplants a year and is second only to Stanford University Hospital as the premier cardiac center in Northern California.

Mercy Hospital

"When I first worked here in 1942, our private rooms, the very best rooms in the house reserved for very special people, went for $12 a week. The semi-private rooms were $6.50, and the beds in the St. Joseph's ward, where our poorer patients stayed, cost $3.25. Well," sighs the speaker, "I don't need to tell you that that was a long time ago."

Sister Mary Daniel is reminiscing about the near half-century she's spent caring for the sick and indigent at Mercy Hospital, the oldest continuing hospital in Sacramento still operating under its original name.

That should perhaps be qualified. Though the Sisters of Mercy have cared for the poor and the socially unfortunate sick in Sacramento for 130 years, their first hospital, which they bought on a $12,000 mortgage note in 1895, was actually called *Mater Misericordiae* Hospital. (The Latin name translates to Mother of Mercy.)

In 1925, Mercy Hospital moved from its original location near Poverty Ridge to its present site at 39th and J streets. Originally the Home of The Merciful Savior, an Episcopa-

lian hospital for the treatment of crippled and invalid children, the hospital which Sister Mary Daniel remembers as Mercy Children's Hospital is now three separate hospitals: Mercy General, Mercy San Juan, and Mercy Folsom, whose 720-bed total capacity is only exceeded by the 843 beds of the three Sutter Health hospitals located in metropolitan Sacramento.

From its J Street headquarters, Mercy expanded by adding a new hospital, Mercy San Juan, in 1953. A third hospital, Mercy Folsom, was added in 1978. They, along with two other branches in Northern California, constitute a comprehensive health care system that still maintains indigent care as an integral part of its mission. "Caring for the poor is very much a part of who we are," says Sister Daniel. "This is why we affiliated with Loaves & Fishes (an organization which donates food to the poor) and established the Norwood walk-in clinic, where we offer free medical care."

Still recognized for its leadership in providing quality medical care for children, Mercy's perinatal program is second only to the one at Sutter Memorial. And in recent years Mercy General has also included a number of new services devoted to outpatient care, like the newly completed, 12-bed out-

patient surgery center.

But to hear Sister Mary Daniel tell it, the specializations that broadened its original scope don't begin to suggest what sets the Mercy system apart. "I think what distinguishes us from the other fine hospitals here in Sacramento isn't the services themselves, but the caring presence of the people who work here."

People like those in the Mercy Guild, a volunteer organization formed in 1953 that provides services and support to Mercy patients, especially the very old and very young. "A good deal of our funding comes from our Guild ladies, and they have contributed a tremendous amount of resources and energy," says Sister Mary Daniel, who came to the hospital in the 1940s as a trainee, left it to teach, and returned as an administrator. "I don't know where we would be without our Guild ladies."

Sister Mary Daniel turns from her visitor, pauses in the lobby stairwell, and nods toward a sepia-toned photo of the three-story, wood-frame structure on R Street where Mercy began. "That, too," she says, "was a long time ago." Her bright eyes twinkle merrily. "Even before my time," she laughs.

From Kaiser to Methodist to Roseville and Beyond

The two local branches of the private-insurance-funded Kaiser system and its esteemed genetic counseling center, Roseville Hospital's excellence in continuing medical education and community health education programs, Methodist Hospital's skilled nursing center, the two Starting Point substance abuse treatment centers, and the seven other hospitals located within the metropolitan area put all parts of the sprawling city within easy reach of a wide array of health care needs and services.

And when the Shriners picked Sacramento as the site of a new children's hospital, it underscored the fact that Sacramento had emerged from health care capital of the valley to major west coast medical center.

Shriners Hospital

In May 1990 the Shriners announced their intent to build a new children's hospital on a 60-acre site between UC Med Center and the old state fairgrounds. The site choice gave new credence to Dr. Loge's statement that Stockton Boulevard was becoming Sacramento's Hospital Row.

The $65-million hospital will be affiliated with the Med Center, and its faculty and the physicians from the Shriners Hospital will work at both hospitals treating spinal cord injuries, burns, and orthopedic needs of kids who now must travel to Galveston, Texas, to receive Shriners care.

Facing page, top: Sutter Center for Psychiatry, holder of several awards for building design, offers a facility that meets the specialized needs of today's psychiatric and mental health care. Photo by Cathy Kelly Architectural Photography

Facing page, bottom: The Sutter Health System provides its patients with an extensive health care network that offers the latest technological advances. Photo by Richard Kaylin

Below: The Mercy hospitals are recognized for their excellent perinatal care. Courtesy, Mercy Health Care, Sacramento

In the spring of 1991, groundbreaking begins on a 300,000-square-foot, 160-bed hospital providing the finest children's medical care that money can't buy. (The Shriners pick up the tab for all the children they treat.) "This is really a great coup for Sacramento," said a delighted Dr. Loge upon receiving the news that the Shriners had chosen Sacramento over the other Northern California sites it considered at the University of San Francisco and Stanford.

The Shriners Hospital will serve an area that stretches west from the Rockies to the Pacific coast, and from the Mexican border to the Canadian line. More than a coup for Sacramento, Shriners Hospital is an acknowledgment and a sign: an acknowledgment of the city's leadership in a field it pioneered throughout its history, and a sign that both recognizes the quality of that leadership and the progressive community which fostered it.

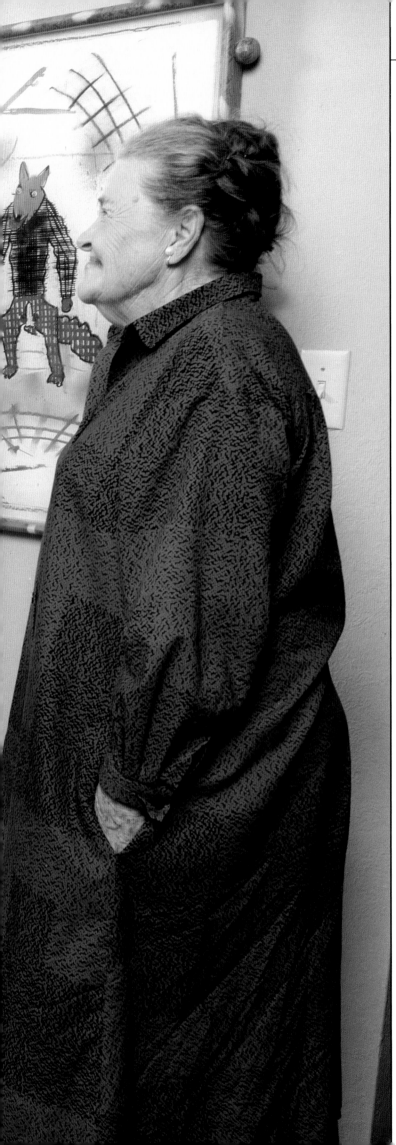

Cultivating the Spirit: The State of the Arts

T| he Crocker:
Sacramento's Grand Dame of the Arts
On a balmy, late summer evening in 1989 a
long stream of dressed-to-the-nines Sacramen-
tans filed up the fan-shaped stairway of a slate-gray Italianate mansion at the corner of Third and O streets. The
Crocker Art Museum, the oldest art museum in America
west of the Mississippi, was about to unveil its new Mansion Wing.

Under construction for a year and a half, the $4.6-
million addition accurately replicates the Second Empire
style of the original home where Judge E.B. and Mrs.
Marguerite Crocker hosted guests like Queen Liliokaulani
of Hawaii and President and Mrs. Ulysses S. Grant.

A parlor room decorated with furnishings from the
Crocker estate recalls that era. The rest of the new wing
houses artwork of a more contemporary mien. Here in
the Friedman and Tsakopoulos Galleries are paintings and
sculptures by the artists who made the rest of the art
world stand up and take notice of the West Coast School:
the revolutionary ceramics of Robert Arneson and David
Gillhooley; the sculpture of Manuel Neri; the paintings of
William Wiley, Ralph Goings, Joseph Raffael, and best
known of all, Wayne Thiebaud, the unassuming master
around whom the Sacramento art scene began forming in
the late 1950s and early 1960s when Thiebaud was teaching full-time at UC Davis.

The Crocker Art Museum, three different wings housing
thirteen separate galleries, a museum shop, a library, and a
ballroom, is primarily known for its contemporary collection
and the Old Master drawings that E.B. and Marguerite col-
lected during a two-year tour of Europe. And while the
Crocker may be the most venerable institution for visual
arts in Sacramento, it is by no means the only show in town.

*The Sacramento area's art scene is thriving with galleries,
museums, and an "Art in Public Places" program. Adeliza
McHugh, director of the Candy Store Gallery in Folsom, is
seen here with artists Robert Arneson (left) and Roy de
Forest. Courtesy, Candy Store Gallery*

Above: Seen here is the Crocker Art Museum, originally the Second Empire style home of Judge E.B. and Marguerite Crocker. Photo by Cathy Kelly Architectural Photography

Right: The Friedman and Tsakopoulos Galleries of the Crocker Art Museum's new wing celebrate paintings and sculpture by contemporary California artists. Photo by Cathy Kelly Architectural Photography

The Gallery Scene

During the early 1960s when Thiebaud, Gladys Neilsen, Jim Nutt, and William Wiley were holding forth to classrooms full of students eager to glean an insight into their own artistic processes, Sacramento began achieving a fair degree of notoriety as an art center. Soon, galleries began sprouting: some like the Candy Store Gallery in out-of-the-way places like Folsom; others like the Open Ring, Jenifer Paul's, and Himovitz galleries in the heart of town.

By the early 1980s, the success of these galleries and the growing stature of Sacramento as a center for visual art gave birth to still more galleries: The Matrix, The Fido, the Artists Contemporary Gallery, and the I.D.E.A. A new art scene based around Friday night art openings came into being as artists and art lovers leapfrogged about town from one gallery to another. Out-of-town collectors soon followed, snapping up the latest work of younger Sacramento artists like Kim Scott, Mick Sheldon, Stephanie Skaliski, Urbano, and Rebecca Gozion.

Some of the locally trained artists followed their mentors, teaching at the local universities and colleges where they

once studied, instructing a new generation of artists and solid-ifying Sacramento's reputation as a locus of west coast art.

So did a vigorous "Art In Public Places" program insti-tuted by the Sacramento Metropolitan Arts Council. Murals soon adorned the sides of banal office buildings, every new high rise seemed destined for a contemporary sculpture, and every light rail stop was festooned with SMAC-funded artwork. You couldn't turn a corner without being SMAC-ed in the face by local art.

Besides the Friday art openings and the annual Kingsley-Crocker exhibition held every April, local artists also dis-played their work in the June "Art Walk" tour, an annual event where artists invite the public into their private stu-dios to observe, inquire, browse, and buy.

Kim Scott, one artist who took part in the "Art Walk," be-lieves it allows the public to acquire a closer understanding of the artists' work: "I think it adds to the work and gives peo-ple a stronger association to the artist as well. It's really fun to be able to share what you do with people who maybe don't have an intimate understanding of art, and I probably gained as much from it as the visitors I entertained."

Part art, part fun, part fashion, the annual Artists Fash-ion Show is another longtime local tradition. Started by artist-poet-musician D.R. Wagner in 1978 when Wagner operated the Open Ring Gallery, the loosely defined

"fashion" show features couture not found at any bou-tique. Usually held in the summer at the Crest Theater, pro-ceeds from the fashion show are now directed to the Sacramento AIDS Foundation.

In Sacramento, the visual arts are more than alive and well; they're ubiquitous, as characteristic a local entity as the softly flowing rivers, the capitol dome, and the summer heat.

The Symphony and the Opera
Inside the Sacramento Community Center Theater the house lights flash and dim. A swirl of strings and oboes essay a note or three and a rising crescendo of applause washes through the hall as the follow spot guides the conductor to the center of the orchestra pit. It's a rainy February eve-ning in the winter of 1990, and the storm outside mirrors the one about to take place within. Conductor Carter Nice taps his baton and the ominous bells of Benjamin Britten's monumental *War Requiem* begin tolling.

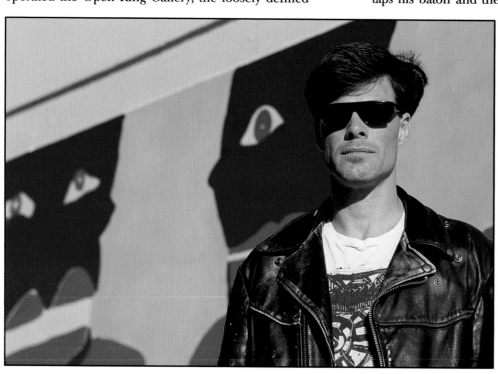

Now in its 78th season, the Sacra-mento Symphony used to be an un-disciplined amalgam of loose-knit afficionados who played in their spare time. That began to change when Maestro Nice left the New Orleans Symphony to accept the Sacramento baton in 1979.

Since then, the symphony's budget has grown from a paltry $500,000 a year to more than $4 million. And its once-dubious musi-cianship has likewise ascended and attracted the notice of San Fran-cisco critics who now concede that an evening of superlative classical music is no longer an exclusive Bay Area preserve. In 1990, one of the symphony's principal soloists, second violinist Sarn Oliver, was invited to perform at the world's

most prestigious classical competition, the once-a-decade-only Tchaikovsky Competition held in Moscow. So much for San Francisco's provincial notions.

Between September and May, the Sacramento Symphony presents 14 classical concerts at the 2,380-seat Community Center Theater, along with six Friday and Saturday pops concerts and seasonal specials like the sing-along *Messiah*, which is quickly becoming a Christmastime tradition in Sacramento.

Though the symphony regularly sells out its subscription, the costs of mounting ever more elaborate programs has exhausted its limited revenue, a sticky situation that once resulted in a musicians' lockout and has been a near annual source of panic for the past half-decade. Finally, in 1990, the city council came to the aid of the beleaguered symphony and provided it with a half-million-dollar appropriation ensuring that Sacramentans' late-blooming passion for classical music could continue unimpeded.

If Sacramento's infatuation with classical music has been an affair that incubated in the bud for eight decades before coming to flower a decade ago, its relationship to the opera has been a romance that came and went and, finally, came again.

Gold Rush miners, shopkeepers, and bankers sat enraptured listening to European stars like Elisa Biscaccianti, Catherine Hayes, and Anna Bishop, whose voices echoed down the Embarcadero streets. But by the middle of this century, opera in Sacramento was a memory. Finally, in 1980, it returned to Sacramento when the newly formed Sacramento Opera Association performed Puccini's *La Boheme*.

It took five years of effort and cajoling before the association put together the requisite funding to stage a full season of opera. Under the hard-driving leadership of General Director Marianne Oaks, that reality eventually came to pass in the fall of 1985.

In its first few years the association's programs were as much miss as hit, and attendance, though enthusiastic, was often sparse. "Those first few years were tough," says Gene Sirois, the association's marketing director. "But we felt it was just a matter of time and audience development. The breakthrough was when we staged a supertitled-version of *Lucia Di Lammermoor* in 1986, and our attendance, once in the 50 percent range, climbed to 97 percent."

The growing support emboldened the opera association, which now mixes staples like Verdi's *Aida* and Puccini's *Tosca* with lesser-known works like Donnizetti's *L'Elisir d'amore* and Gounod's *Faust*. San Francisco reviewers, again stunned that their seeming monopoly on high culture was

Above: Sacramento's performing arts associations, such as the ballet, the symphony, and the opera, play to appreciative crowds at the Sacramento Community Center Theater. Photo by Tom Myers

Facing page, top: Renowned artist Wayne Thiebaud and his son Matt Bult share a proud moment at the Michael Himovitz Gallery during a show of their work. Photo by Owen Brewer, courtesy, The Sacramento Bee

Facing page, bottom: Artist Steve Vanoni stands before his colorful mural adorning the side of the Sequoia Pacific Warehouse building, which houses the Sacramento History Museum. The artist was a winner in a contest that was part of the "Art in Public Places" program, sponsored by the Sacramento Metropolitan Arts Commission. Photo by Richard Kaylin

less fact than myth, came to scorn and left to praise. As the *Examiner*'s Richard Pontzious wrote: "Until yesterday, I had ignored the Sacramento Opera . . . now I know that was a mistake . . . There's a future for opera in Sacramento, and I, for one, will look forward to spending time there."

The Ballet and Broadway Road Shows

Sacramento's tendency is to effect a laid-back and casual appearance. Getting dressed for an evening out used to mean a fresh pair of Levis and a new t-shirt. But black-tie and strings-of-pearls no longer rouses the cocked eyebrows it once did. The elegantly dressed, packed houses for the symphony and opera at the Community Center reflect this. As do the equally well-turned-out crowds attending the ballet and the Broadway touring shows that share the same stage.

Now in its 35th year, the Sacramento Ballet was founded by Barbara Crocket-Gallo back in 1955. A true believer, Crocket-Gallo operated the company until 1988 when she handed the reins to current artistic director Ron Cunningham.

Sacramento was fortunate to get Cunningham, who previously served as principal dancer, choreographer, and ballet master with the Boston Ballet. Alternating classic pieces with his more daring original work, Cunningham,

Left: Puccini's La Fanciulla del West *(The Girl of the Golden West) is one of the few western operas ever written. This production by the Sacramento Opera Association featured two live horses on stage during the last act for authenticity. Photo by Roger Ele, courtesy, the Sacramento Opera Association*

Facing page: Maggie Marshall as Adriane Utterword and Joe Vincent as Hector Hushabye take the stage in the Sacramento Theater Company's production of George Bernard Shaw's Heartbreak House. *Courtesy, The Sacramento Theater Company*

Below left: Members of the Sacramento Ballet wait in the wings before taking center stage. This venerable arts institution has achieved acclaim under the leadership of artistic director Ron Cunningham. Photo by Tom Myers

along with the Phares Ballet and Nolan T'Sani of the now-defunct Capitol Ballet, helped lift ballet into prominence in the cultural firmament of Sacramento.

Though most often hosting concerts, arias, or grand jetés, the main stage of the Community Center is rarely dark. It is here, on off-nights, where the touring companies of *Cats, Phantom of the Opera, Big River,* or the other half-dozen Broadway roadshows that visit Sacramento each year stage their productions.

In a sense, these productions, along with the Community Center seminars and visiting lecture series, attest to Sacramento's growing stature as an emerging cultural center on the west coast. Native Sacramentan Maurice Read says: "It seems only yesterday that anytime you wanted to go out for an evening's entertainment, you had to go to the Bay Area. Now there's so much to do that you agonize when you have to make a choice. In less than a decade we've gone from light fare to a moveable feast."

Theater

Edwin Booth, James O'Neill, Bert Lahr, the entire Barrymore clan, and Tallulah Bankhead—these marquee names of the theater all trod Sacramento's boards at one time or another. More recently, actors like Tom Hanks, Timothy Busfield, Molly Ringwald, and Olivia Brown either got their start in Sacramento or studied here before moving on to New York or Hollywood. In Busfield's case, *thirtysomething*'s Elliot continues to maintain a local presence with his Fantasy Children's Theater. Brown recently opened a nightclub —"Miss Olivia's"—in Old Sacramento.

In a recent essay, *Sacramento Bee* theater critic Peter Haugen wrote that some people look at theater in Sacramento as a glass half-empty, while others see it as a glass half-full.

Another way of looking at it is as a glassworks whose vessels come in a variety of shapes and styles; from the big to the small, from the trad to the rad, and a whole lot of in-between.

There are currently some 30 theater groups operating in the four-county Sacramento metropolitan area, including the Music Circus, a longtime summer favorite which recently celebrated its 35th year and is just what its name implies—big-time Broadway musicals with big-time box-office names staged under a Big Top—to the avant-garde work of the Chautauqua Theater, the Elly-award-winning Show Below, and the Sacramento Theater Company's "Cutting Edge" series.

The flagship of this piebald fleet is the Sacramento Theater Company (STC), founded in 1942 as the Sacramento Civic Theater by Eleanor McClatchy, the late publisher/editor of the *Sacramento Bee* (the aforementioned Elly award is named in her honor).

Since then, STC has undergone more transformations than Proteus. Actress and acting teacher Miriam Gray-Duffy,

an STC veteran who witnessed many of those changes, recalls that tumultuous period: "When I first started acting with STC, it was then called EMPAC—the Eleanor McClatchy Performing Arts Center—because it did everything from straight theater to children's theater to ballet to you name it. And though it was the most professional theater company in town, none of the actors or directors got paid. Now almost all theaters pay their directors, and many of them—like Garbeau's Dinner Theater out in Nimbus Winery—also pay their actors."

Instead of its former theatrical incarnation as all things to all theatergoers, STC now presents a varied program of drama combining warhorses like G.B. Shaw's *Heartbreak House* and Dickens' *Christmas Carol* with more contemporary dramas like David Mamet's *Glengarry Glen Ross* and Alfred Uhry's *Driving Miss Daisy.*

Garbeau's Dinner Theater, the aforementioned 250-seat space in the Nimbus Winery off Highway 50 past Rancho Cordova, favors lighter fare like Noel Coward and Neil Simon comedies, Agatha Christie whodunits, and light musicals. The other 20-odd theaters dotting metropolitan Sacramento are a mixed-bag, from the student productions at the colleges and universities, to the Fair Oaks and Land Park Summer Shakespeare series, to open-ended performance art and avant-garde pieces at venues like the recently refurbished Guild Theater in Oak Park.

In years to come Sacramento theater will likely undergo a winnowing-out process as larger troupes like STC move from their 300-seat home at the Eleanor McClatchy Center to a much larger venue more befitting their status, while the cream of the rest of the crop vacate the temporary spaces many of them now occupy and move into new theaters currently being planned.

More importantly, Sacramento will also see the creation of a theater district between the just-refurbished 2,500-seat Memorial Auditorium at 16th and J streets and the Sacramento Theater Company's present home at 14th and H streets.

"What we hope to do is create a series of public-private partnerships by offering developers incentives to do this through zoning tradeoffs," says Gene Masuda, one of the chief architects for the Downtown Cultural and Entertainment District Master Plan. Masuda sees the creation of Theater Row as yet another piece in the puzzle to transform Sacramento into a 24-hour city. "Theater Row is one piece, but so is Museum Mile."

As part of the master plan, adopted in 1990, Museum Mile will create two new museum spaces between the long-derelict PG&E power station north of Old Sacramento on

The largest museum of its kind in North America, the California State Railroad Museum at Second and I streets evokes the days of train travel with 21 restored trains and 46 exhibits. Photo by Cathy Kelly Architectural Photography.

the Jibboom Street levee, and the already existing Towe Ford Museum to the south at Front & V streets.

Just underway, the PG&E renovation will transform the landmark power plant which once supplied the entire city with electricity into a museum chronicling the history of the massive California Water Project. Moving south along the river, "Museum Mile" calls for an expansion of Old Town's California Railroad Museum—the largest museum of its kind in the United States—with an adjacent hall dedicated to railroad technology. And with renovation already underway at the nearby Southern Pacific site, the downtown Sacramento of the 1990s will be bookended by Theater Row on the east and Museum Mile's Railroad Row on the west.

Music Festivals

Just before the Memorial Day weekend, they begin rolling into town. They come in campers, in Winnebagos, in limousines, Model T's, and on motorcycle. They come from every state of the union, from every country in the free world, and from behind what used to be the Iron Curtain before *glasnost* rang it down. By early April, every hotel room in town has been booked for weeks, and gleeful shopkeepers have rubbed their palms raw. It's a friendly inva-

sion that Sacramento has welcomed annually since 1974, the year the Dixeland Jubilee first began.

Legend has it that the idea was born at an after-hours jam when one traditional jazz player turned to another and said "You know, what we ought to do is start a jazz festival in Old Town."

The story is probably apocryphal. But in the 17 years since its inception, the jazz bash has continued to grow in size and stature until it now encompasses seven regional sites all over town: from the El Rancho Hotel across the river in West Sacramento to its Old Town birthplace; from Cal Expo to the Music Circus tent; and at almost every available stage in between.

Phil Harris, Wild Bill Davidson, Teddy Wilson, and the late Earl "Fatha" Hines are a few of the greats who have graced the Jubilee's roster, which annually presents 80 or so traditional jazz acts to more than 100,000 attendees. Jim Jones, editor of *And All That Jazz*, the official Dixieland Jazz Society newsletter, recalls the early days when the festival drew 8,000 in a good year: "I can't really explain why it took off like it did. It just seems that there's something about the flavor of this area that people are very drawn to."

Though it's by far the most widely attended of all Sacramento's music festivals, Dixieland is not every jazz lover's cup of tea. And by the mid-1980s Sacramentans eager for a taste of something a bit more "outside" began staging their own summer concert series at McClatchy Park.

Since its inception in 1985, the free summer concerts in the heart of Oak Park have booked some of the most

Right: This tuba player is part of the musical revels to be experienced at the Dixieland Jubilee. Photo by Tom Myers

Facing page, left: A guide dressed like a nineteenth-century station master entertains and educates visitors at the California State Railroad Museum. Photo by Mark Gibson

Facing page, right: Costumed docents at Sutter's Fort demonstrate the use of antique firearms for visitors. The frontier museum has been reconstructed on the original site where John Augustus Sutter settled in 1839. Photo by George Elich

storied names in bebop, post-bop, and avant-garde jazz. Dizzy Gillespie, Clark Terry, Nancy Wilson with the Louie Bellson Orchestra, and Phil Woods have been recent performers at the four-concerts-a-year Oak Park Concert Series sponsored by the *Sacramento Bee*'s "Summer in the City" program. The Oak Park concerts rely more on word-of-mouth publicity than on direct advertising. And though the crowds may only number in the hundreds, this series isn't about mass, it's about musical quality.

Though locals' appetite for jazz is demonstrable through their attendance at the Dixieland Jubilee and the Oak Park events, the other musical form most dear to Sacramentans' hearts is the blues.

Held at the end of September, the annual Blues Festival is staged at the same site as the Jubilee. All similarities end there. The Jubilee is the product of a well-oiled machine that draws upon hundreds of volunteers; the Blues Festival is pretty much a one-man operation.

When Phil Givant, a professor of mathematics at American River College, started the festival in 1976, it was held on the lawn of the college and attended by maybe 500 students. The next year Givant moved the festival to William Land Park. The year after that he expanded it to a two-day affair. Then after a brief stay at Hughes Stadium, Givant moved the festival to its present site, where it's been for the past decade.

The Blues Festival unofficially marks the end of the summer festival season in Sacramento and locals and out-of-towners alike take advantage of the still-balmy weather to come and bask in the sun, swim in the rivers, and enjoy some of the hottest blues this side of Beale or Bourbon streets.

John Lee Hooker, Little Milton, Albert Collins, Johnny Winter, Buddy Guy, and Lonnie Mack are some of the headliners who have appeared at recent blues fests. And if Givant has his way, the broad range of available styles will

expand in the future: "I'd even book a rap group, if I found the right group that could make the connection between rap and blues."

While Givant was indulging his passion for all forms of the blues, another professor at CSUS was honing his plan to create a music festival unlike any other on the west coast.

Music professor Gene Savage wanted to combine the best of American contemporary classical music in a forum that was both instructive and entertaining, and with that in mind Savage created the Festival of New American Music in 1978.

Using lectures, seminars, master classes, and informal get-togethers as well as concert performances, the New American Music Festival provides a forum for some of America's more adventurous artists to explore music's outer realms in a campus setting.

The 10-day free festival has lately begun to gain national attention for its unique and eclectic flavor, where one can hear everything from the post-bop jazz of saxophonist Harold Land to the boundary-defying Kronos Quartet to the more traditional Debussy Trio. An early November event, the new American Music Festival is probably the least-attended of Sacramento's music fests. But those who do attend don't feel short-changed.

"In terms of pure musical significance, this is easily the most important festival in Sacramento," says Steve Passarell, drummer with Bub, a local avant-garde jazz quintet. "Where else am I going to find Harold Land playing one night, a premiere of a new piece by Terry Reilly on another, and a string quartet composition seminar the next afternoon?"

Club and Concert Venues

When David Bowie made Sacramento's Cal Expo Amphitheater one of three California stops on his 1990 tour, a subtle yet important message was essentially being delivered: Sacramento was now *definitely* on the map for major touring acts.

The Bowie concert, as well as other 1990 appearances by Robert Plant, the Allman Brothers Band, and Anita Baker, were all produced by San Francisco legend Bill Graham, the impressario of the late, lamented Fillmore who has lately expanded his presence in Sacramento, adding four to five dates a year to his Nissan-sponsored summer concert series.

Besides the Graham-Nissan productions, additional concerts produced by LB Presentations have brought stars like Harry Connick, Jr., and Grover Washington to the Community Center Theater. The Crest Theater on K Street tends toward cutting-edge rock'n'roll headliners, and the Radisson Hotel presents acts like k.d. lang, Chris Isaak, and Jean-Luc Ponty at its lovely outdoor amphitheater.

As seems always to be the case when a city experiences the kind of dynamic growth that Sacramento has, the last place that growth is manifested is at the nightclub level.

For the past two decades local club scene denizens have heard that it was "about to happen" in Sacramento and have been left hanging as to when it would. In the early 1980s, it didn't look too promising when a number of nightspots like The China Wagon, the Club Can't Tell, The I-Dream Cafe, and the Oasis Ballroom closed their doors. The nightclub neon grew dim.

"I think grim is probably a better description," says Bob Cheevers, the Nashville-raised singer/songwriter and 20-year veteran of the local club scene. "It seems to come and go in waves, and I've seen about three different crests and troughs since I moved here."

But by the tail end of the 1980s the trough had reached its bottom and the crest began to swell again. Downtown clubs like On Broadway, the Hyatt's Busby Berkeley's, the Metro, Miss Olivia's, Melarkey's, The Cattle Club, J.R.'s, and Drago's opened up and started programming progressive music, while country was king out in northeastern Sacramento clubs like The Yellow Rose, Nashville West, and the Country Comfort Lounge. A fairly substan-

tial mainstream music scene also began to swell at the Hilton's Pink Cadillac, Roseville's Classic Juke Box, and Charley Brown's.

The club scene renaissance carried over to restaurants as well. Andaimo's, Aldo's, Rickey's, and the Bull Market began booking light jazz while Tango's could boast the superlative pianist Jessica Williams.

"About to happen" Sacramento woke up to find that it was in fact happening.

Festas, Fairs, and Festivals

Every June in the river village of Freeport, a colorful procession of flags and banners and young girls draped in robes of royal blue proceeds from the I.D.E.S. Portuguese hall to St. Mary's Catholic Church in Courtland. After services, they make the four-mile journey back. Thus another two-day Festa begins.

Facing page, top: Seniors parade to the rhythms of jazz during the Dixieland Jubilee. Begun in 1974, the festival has reached huge proportions, spreading out to seven sites throughout the city and attracting visitors from around the world. Photo by George Elich

Facing page, bottom: Tempting the adventurous palate, steamed crawfish are among the culinary offerings of the Isleton Crawdad Festival, one of the Delta's summer food celebrations. Photo by Tom Myers

Below: Sacramento's various ethnic festivals are evidence of the community's rich cultural diversity. Photo by Tom Myers

or baked in pies—wafts up to greet you and the other 125,000 in attendance.

The next month, it's the Courtland Pear Fair and the Dixon Lamb Fest. The feasting continues in Sacramento with August's Japanese Buddhist Fair and the Italian Food Festival. The next month it's the Greek Food Fair. The month after that, it's the Armenian Fair. If you make them all, you're probably a likely candidate for Jenny Craig.

But the festival that native Sacramentans most cherish celebrates neither national background nor edible commodity but rather the flower that is the city's symbol: the camellia.

Held in early March, the Camellia Festival celebrated its 35th year in 1990. And though some think the festival has wilted a bit of late, it still remains one of *the* social events of the year, especially the formal dress cocktail and dinner finale, the Camellia Ball.

The festival allows Sacramento's avid and amateur gardeners a chance to show off the magnificent multicolored blooms that have been the city's official flower since 1941. It begins with a Land Park bike race sponsored by the Capital City Wheelmen, the local bicycle club founded in the nineteenth century, and then moves downtown for a parade around Capitol Park. The festival then moves inside, to the Community Center Exhibit Hall, where more than 5,000 pink, red, and white camellias are put on display. Hundreds of prizes are available, allowing even the most novice horticulturalists a chance of winning.

Nearly 100 years old, the Portuguese Festival of the Holy Spirit is the first of the summer fairs hosted on the Delta. And though its inspiration is religious rather than agricultural, like all Delta festivals it includes an open-to-the-public feast of epic proportions.

The Isleton Crawdad Festival follows the Portuguese fair a couple weeks later. If you close your eyes and open your nostrils, you might think you're in the Louisiana Delta as the smells of grilled alligator, or crawfish—steamed, stuffed,

Though the richness of Sacramento's cultural life has struggled to keep pace with the city's growth, the days when the old local saying, "It's pretty good—for Sacramento" held the currency it once did are now past.

Miriam Gray-Duffy, the flame-topped actress and acting teacher, sees Sacramento's cultural energy as "both dynamic *and* low-key," the kind of environment that "allows you to take a break from your craft, move away from it for awhile, and return to it when you've recharged."

Playtime in River City

S|**ports for All Seasons**
● At Renfree Park on a hot summer's night, a sharp thwack echoes through the milky air and a baseball, lucent white as it tracks above the floodlit field, dims to gray and fades out of sight beyond the fence in the cobalt darkness. Sacramento's aging Boys of Summer are at it again.

● A crisp Saturday morning along the American River Parkway in early fall finds John Smith on a bicycle halfway to Folsom from his house on Garden Highway near the parkway's end. When he completes the 22.5-mile jaunt, his wife Debra and son Richard will be waiting for him in his Datsun pickup to drive him back. Though other, more serious, cyclists pass him on the bike trail, Smith is unperturbed by considerations of speed and time, concentrating instead on the canvas he's been commissioned to paint and how he can incorporate the smear of bright fall colors into the piece.

● The winter tule fog hangs in the cottonwoods guarding the tricky approach to William Land Park's nightmarish third hole. *Sacramento Magazine* writer and self-confessed golf addict Dennis Pottenger selects a 6-iron and essays his lie. Drawing a bead on the barely visible flag, Pottenger shoots into the mist. A chattering sound precedes a switch of falling cottonwood, followed by the soft plunk of the Slazenger #1. The ball has traveled all of 30 yards. "One of these days," Pottenger mutters, "I'm gonna beat these stupid trees and get down in three."

● The black water plashes gently and oarlocks click and groan as the CSUS crew team cuts through the still water of Lake Natoma on an achingly clear April day. Hearing their approach, five white egrets and a single blue heron flap their heavy wings, lift off the lake, and fly out of harm's way to fish in the marshy shallows.

Every August, Cal Expo's 600-acre grounds are home to the California State Fair, an event that features exciting rides such as the one seen here. Photo by Bob Rowan/ Progressive Image Photography

Pro Sports:
From the Solons to the Kings
At the corner of Broadway and Riverside Boulevard directly opposite the history-rich Sacramento City Cemetery, on a lot now occupied by a Target department store, there once stood a rickety old stadium that represented the pinnacle of professional sports in Sacramento.

Edmonds Field, formerly Doubleday Park, and before that Cardinal Field, was the home of the beloved and late-lamented Sacramento Solons, the Pacific Coast League Triple A farm team of what was then the Milwaukee Braves.

For 40 years, Edmonds Field entertained Sacramento's rabid baseball fans. But when the franchise was sold, the park's days were numbered. In 1964 Edmonds Field, and its magnificent "Casey at the Bat" mural that greeted fans as they passed through its turnstile, were bulldozed.

Gregg Lukenbill was six years old when his father took him to see his first Solons game. He came away enraptured: "It was the smells of the hot peanuts and steamed hot dogs, and the way the crowd would start to buzz when they sensed a rally was about to happen. Just the entire experience of being there, really. Man, I'll tell you, I was hooked from then on."

Hooked enough to think he could bring professional sports back to Sacramento, enraptured and driven enough to actually pull it off.

"Everybody thought me and my partners father Frank, fellow developers Joe and Richard Benvenuti and Bob Cook, and realtor Steve Cippa were lunatics when we first proposed building a stadium to attract a professional sports franchise."

The first site that Lukenbill and company proposed was on Bradshaw Road at Highway 50 near Rancho Cordova. It didn't fly. Then, in 1979, Lukenbill tried again, proposing a more accessible location at the junction of Interstates

Such are the sights, the sounds, the rhythms of the season reflected at these and hundreds of other stations of sporting and recreational activity scattered across metropolitan Sacramento.

From winter skiing in the nearby Sierras to summer water sports. From organized leagues at manicured fields to pick-up games on asphalt playgrounds. From the skilled professional athlete plying his trade to the tune of millions to the most amateur of duffers, hackers, and maybe-try-it-oncers out for a lark. From Galt to North Natomas, from Folsom to Davis and all points in between, at any given moment, on any given day at any time of the year, Sacramentans are out there with bat, ball, racket, fin, or club—Just Doing It, as the Nike ads say.

Above and Left: The Sacramento Kings, the first major league franchise in Sacramento, play to sell-out crowds at the 17,500-seat Arco Arena. Photo by Rocky Widner, courtesy, The Sacramento Kings

Facing page: Cyclists enjoy the bike paths along the American River Parkway. Photo by Mark Gibson

5 and 880 in what were then the rice fields of North Natomas. Again, he was hammered. The city council, led by Mayor Philip Isenberg, opposed the plan. Lukenbill did manage to get a stadium bond measure on that year's ballot, but voters turned it down.

So Lukenbill waited until 1982, when Isenberg and fellow councilmember and stadium opponent Lloyd Connelly left city hall for seats in the state assembly. Then he made his move.

First he acquired a floundering NBA franchise, buying the Kansas City Kings for $10.5 million in 1983.

In 1985, Lukenbill built a temporary stadium and moved the Kings into it. That done, he began construction on a permanent home at nearby Arco Arena, completing it in time for the start of the 1988 season.

Ever since then the Kings have played to capacity crowds at the 17,500-seat arena. The sellouts are based more on the city's enthusiasm for the sport than on the team's performance. The Kings did manage to make it to the first round of the playoffs at the end of their inaugural season, but they've been perennial doormats of the rugged Pacific Division ever since.

After three chaotic seasons of management and coaching changes and questionable personnel moves, Lukenbill decided he'd seen enough. Sensing there was a limit to Kings

fans' patience, Lukenbill hired one of the winningest coaches in NBA history and gave him near-total control of the team.

The hiree was Dick Motta, the discipline-minded basketball fundamentalist who'd guided winning franchises at Dallas, Chicago, and Washington. To his credit, Motta didn't bemoan the weak hand he'd been given when taking reign of the Kings in November 1989. But any doubt of what he *really* thought about the ragtag assemblage of talent that sometimes shined individually but hardly resembled a *team* was removed when the season concluded.

Motta decided to build from scratch. Swapping almost

Above: Cycling is a way of life in Sacramento and races are very popular. Here participants in the Coors Classic round the bend near Capitol Mall. Photo by Tom Myers

Facing page: Tennis courts are common features of planned communities such as this one near Laguna Lake. A mild year-round climate gives Sacramento's tennis afficionados an almost unlimited opportunity to play. Photo by Tom Myers

Left: The brain child of Sacramentan Gregg Lukenbill, the Arco Arena, located at One Sports Parkway, is home to the Sacramento Kings. Photo by Richard Kaylin

all the proven veterans on the roster for draft picks, the Kings made history on Draft Day, 1990, by becoming the first team in NBA history to have four first-round picks.

Whether or not the Motta-led children's crusade can storm the NBA battlements and secure the playoff berth the Kings have been denied since their maiden season is problematical. But the housecleaning has been enthusiastically received by the team's fans, if not the local media.

Sacramento's "Sweet Science" Practitioners

Waiting on the Kings to capture a sporting crown at some future date wasn't good enough for those less patient Sacramento fans who wanted to see their civic pride immediately reflected through sporting excellence. "Give us a winner" was the war chant that went up at Arco

Arena. "Give us a champion."

Their hunger was soon appeased. And when that sought-for championship came, it came from the sport that some pundit dubbed "the sweet science," a misnomer of sorts, because the sport itself is anything *but* sweet: 12 to 15 rounds of sweat, pain, and fury in the sheer hell of a squared circle—boxing.

Sacramento has always been a great fight town. Visited by early champions John L. Sullivan and James J. Corbett who staged exhibition matches along the Embarcadero, the city had its first champion in the 1930s when local product Max Baer, Sr., briefly held the heavyweight crown before relinquishing it to the great Joe Louis.

In the 1960s, Sacramento's Joey Lopes made a long run at the middleweight crown before Carl "Bobo" Olsen put an end to his dream. And in the 1970s, a CSUS student named Pete Ranzany flirted with welterweight title hopes until champion Pipino Cuevas doused his lights one windy night at Hughes Stadium before the hometown crowd even had a chance to get seated.

In the early 1980s, it was featherweight Bobby Chacon who raised local fight fans' hopes. Chacon won a crown but lost it shortly thereafter. Beset by personal problems, he soon retired.

But on a warm July evening in 1988, Sacramentans were finally rewarded when a totally relentless and fearless mighty mite of a man named Tony Lopez wrested the undisputed junior lightweight crown from champion "John-John" Molina.

They call him "Tony the Tiger," partly due to the fact that he wears tiger-striped boxing trunks, partly because he has the heart of a jungle cat. But mostly it's because of his ferocity.

That July night at Arco Arena, Lopez's fans were treated to a particularly tiger-ish performance. Lopez waded through Molina's textbook jabs and counters, willing to absorb the punishment they delivered in order to get inside where he is most effective.

By the fifth round, Lopez's left eye was moused to an ugly, red slit. But by the tenth round, the Tiger's devastating barrage to Molina's body had turned the champ's legs to jelly. A left-right-left combination late in the round put Molina on the deck. Molina gamely rose at eight and finished the last two rounds, vainly trying to fend off Lopez, who mauled him about the ring like a cat toying with a rag doll full of cat-nip.

The judge's decision was almost an after-thought. Tony the Tiger raised the gold-encrusted International Boxing Federation belt above his head, and the city went berserk, whooping it up at longtime fight game bastions like The Torch Club and Melarkey's. And though, like Chacon, an out-of-condition Tony would lose his crown back to Molina in a rematch the next year, he came back to take the rubber match in convincing fashion.

Then, in the summer of 1990, Sacramento had its second native-born boxing champion when junior welterweight Loreto Garza decisioned Juan Coggia in Nice, France. An occasional sparring partner of Lopez, Garza's victory cemented Sacramento's claim to boxing excellence. "Winning a world title is something I've always dreamed of," Garza said after the fight. "Now I'm looking forward to defending the title before the home fans at Arco."

Baseball: A Longtime Local Passion

Long before there even was an Edmonds Field or a Sacramento Solons, baseball was a local mania. Alexander Cartwright, who laid out the dimensions of the present baseball diamond and codified many of the sports' rules, organized Sacramento's first baseball team during the Gold Rush. And in the mid-nineteenth century the mania manifested itself when Sacramento's many breweries fielded semi-pro teams at local baseball diamonds like Snowflake Park and Exhibition Field.

Amateur baseball flourished. And over the years, the city's mild springs, long hot summers, and dry autumns would prove a conducive environment to producing some of the best professional baseball talent of any city in the country.

Dusty Baker, Larry Bowa, Bob and Ken Forsch, Leron and Leon Lee, and Butch Metzgar were the first generation of local stars to make a major impact at the professional level. Some of the more recognizable Sacramento stars still enjoying professional baseball careers include the

Yankees' Steve Sax, the Phillies' Rickey Jordan, the Angels' Max Venable, and the Brewers' Chris Bosio and Gregg Vaughan.

"Sacramento is probably the best baseball environment of any city on the west coast," claims Greg Van Dusen, vice president of the Sacramento Sports Association, "and we've made a commitment to getting a franchise here by the end of the '90s."

Gregg Lukenbill's zest for another sports franchise nearly landed him in hot water when a San Francisco grand jury indicted him and four others for attempting to influence a San Francisco ballot measure that proposed building a new baseball stadium in downtown San Francisco. "It was a witch-hunt, and they were looking for a convenient scapegoat," said a relieved Lukenbill when the charges were finally

Above: A speedboat, pulling a water skier performing slalom maneuvers, cuts through the sparkling waters of Folsom Lake. Photo by Dick Schmidt, courtesy, The Sacramento Bee

Left: Residents of the Rancho Murieta subdivision, a closed community located along the Cosumnes River east of Sacramento, enjoy the use of a private lake. Photo by Kent Lacin

Facing page: Thrill seekers looking for the ultimate white water experience need look no further than the turbulent rapids of the American River. Photo by Mark Gibson

dropped. "It won't slow me down a bit."

But even if Sacramento doesn't achieve Lukenbill's desire of seeing a major league franchise locate at Arco Park, baseball is very much a part of the local sports scene. Whether it's the ex-major leaguers like Butch Metzgar and Sammy Lovelace still lacing 'em up at Renfree Park, or the 4,000 softball teams that represent 40,000 players who participate in summer league play at the 108 baseball diamonds in the metropolitan area, baseball remains one of Sacramento's primary summer recreation options.

Golf and Tennis

For Sacramento's other professional sports franchise, the World Team Tennis league's Sacramento Capitals, the story

so far has been "close but no cigar."

Playing their seven home matches at the prestigious Gold River Racket Club located along the American River near Folsom, the Capitals have treated their followers to winning seasons since first arriving on the scene in 1986. Yet every year during the playoffs, the Capitals have come away empty.

Their chief nemesis has been the San Antonio Racquets, a team the Capitals have twice challenged for the $450,000 championship and lost.

The Capitals draw a devoted following that nearly fills Gold River's 2,000-seat stadium from the thousands of amateurs who play at Sacramento's private clubs like Arden Hills, Sutter Lawn, and Rio del Oro as well as the 18 court complexes open to the public. "We're developing a very strong community base," says Capitals spokesperson Bev Kindrick. "What we'd like to see is one of our young local players develop to become a member of this team."

Golf is another local sports obsession. Thirty thousand local players tee up daily at the 18 private and public links

Right: It's six stories straight down for those who brave "The Cliff Hanger" slide at Waterworld, a theme park located on the California State Fairgrounds. Photo by Tom Myers

Facing page, top: This lion and her cub are residents of the 15-acre Sacramento Zoo located in William Land Park. Photo by Jeff Burckhard/Life Images

Facing page, bottom: Once the most popular annual event in Sacramento, the California State Fair fell on hard times in the sixties and seventies. Recently, however, the attraction has regained its former stature. Photo by Tom Myers

in metropolitan Sacramento. "The worst part about it," says Dennis Pottenger, "is the waiting you have to do when you do get a tee time. We're stretched beyond capacity. We need more golf courses. It's almost become too popular."

That popularity is most evident in August when the PGA Senior Gold Rush tour comes to town. Now in its fifth year, the $500,000 event is staged 20 miles east of Sacramento at the Rancho Murieta Country Club. The sloping foothill course, which lines the bank of the Cosumnes River, has challenged the likes of Arnold Palmer, Lee Trevino, and crowd favorite Chi-Chi Rodriguez, who took home the $50,000 winner's check in 1988.

Amateur Athletics: From the Pigbowl to the Causeway

During the summer and fall of 1989, Sacramentans witnessed an ongoing drama pitting two of America's more visible sports mavericks, Sacramento Kings owner Gregg Lukenbill and Los Angeles Raiders owner Al Davis. The drama unfolded over the Raiders' destiny. Davis wanted to move the Raiders, and Lukenbill wanted the Raiders to move to Sacramento. Given the two headstrong personalities involved, it was hardly surprising that the deal came undone.

Before Sacramento got the Surge, its new World League of American Football franchise, it had to satisfy its football appetite with the Pig Bowl and the Causeway Classic.

Beginning in 1973, the annual Pig Bowl was initially a public relations gesture by the Sacramento Police Department and the Sacramento County Sheriff's Office to cool the still hot temperatures of social unrest. (The event draws its name from the epithet that was daily hurled at police officers during that period.)

The Pig Bowl is now one of Sacramento's biggest charity events. The proceeds from the January game are set aside for the Sacramento Children's Home.

The Causeway Classic is more of a blood feud along the order of the Hatfields and McCoys. The Cal State Sacramento Hornets occupy the Sacramento side of the causeway while the UC Davis Aggies are on the Yolo side. And every year, the two square off in a football game that determines bragging rights.

Cycling, Boating, Fishing, Skiing

As soon as the rainy season ends in March, and sometimes even before then, Sacramento's avid cyclists take to the 300 miles of bike trails that wind along the levee banks of the Sacramento and American rivers and through many of the city's parks and streets.

Cycling is more than a local tradition (the Capital City Wheelmen, the first city bike club, was formed in 1886), it's

a way of life, as the nearby city of Davis confirms.

Sacramento may not be as bike-crazed as Davis is. No-body is. In Davis, the number of bikes actually exceeds the population. Still, Sacramento isn't very far behind. And the regional cycling fervor is mirrored by a number of competitions held in the summer months.

The biggest is the Nevada City Classic, a 100-miler in which cyclists rip along the Victorian-lined streets of that Gold Rush town. The longest is the 200-mile Davis to

Napa Valley race held a month earlier. But by far the most popular cycling event is "Eppie's Great Race," the Sacramento event held in July that attracted a record 2,000 participants in 1990.

Technically, it's a triathalon, the world's oldest, in fact. Started by Sacramento restauranteur Eppie Johnson in 1974, the meet begins and ends at Goethe Park on the American River.

Cycling appeals to Sacramento's more fitness-minded folks. But the hot summer days and the lassitude they can induce cause others to seek less strenuous sports, though to hear Mark Molin tell it there's nothing more exerting than trying to hook a salmon, shad, or steelhead.

When the mercury heads north, Molin heads south from his Land Park home to "Minnow Hole," the fishing spot that he and maybe 30 other angling army regulars

Vividly painted rides at the California State Fair form a pleasing visual medley. Photo by Bob Rowan/Progressive Image Photography

occupy from May until October.

"Hardest sport in the world, hooking a salmon," Molin says, a facetious grin on his face. "Yeah, it's a tough job, but, well, somebody's got to do it," he cackles, throwing cast after ceaseless cast into the Sacramento River.

Steelhead season follows the summer salmon run. Then it's on to stripers and shad in the spring as Molin moves north up the Sacramento to its confluence with the Feather.

But the big trophy fish are down the Delta near the San Pablo Bay where 400-pound prehistoric sturgeon lurk. "You get a sturgeon, then you're *really* talkin' exercise," warns Minnow Hole Molin, throwing one last dusk-time cast toward the "v" of the current where a salmon jumped three hours before. "See what I mean? Tough job." He pauses a moment. "*Real* tough job."

You can fish the rivers. You can float them, a favorite summer option for the thousands of Sacramentans who take the all-day journey between Sunrise Bridge and Discovery Park where the American meets the Sacramento. If it's thrills you're after, there's always the white water of the American on either its north or south forks. Or you can ski them, and if you're good enough at it you might be one of the 800 water skiers receiving an invitation to compete at the U.S. Nationals held at Bell's Aqua water park in the suburb of Rio Linda. You can swim them, kayak or canoe them, or glide atop them on a sailboard. But if you're lucky enough, you might even get to live on them.

George Bruder, a counselor at Christian Brothers High School, is one of the lucky 5,000 river dwellers berthed at the 20 marinas between Sacramento and Isleton.

Bruder now leads as laid-back a life-style as possible. But it took a fair amount of labor to arrive there. It took him two years to build his houseboat, but he says it was well worth the effort. "My job can get pretty stressful, and I need a release from it. There's a serenity here that's very calming and it helps me do my work knowing I have this to come home to."

When the tule fog drapes its moist gray blanket over the valley, and the hard rains of December drive the less hardy indoors, many Sacramento sports enthusiasts simply head to the hills.

To the slopes of the Sierras, actually. For here, within a

two-and-a-half-hour drive of Sacramento, is where you'll find some of the world's finest winter skiing.

Thirteen different downhill resorts and six cross-country facilities lie within easy reach of Sacramento and offer skiers a variety of choices, from the demanding chutes of Heavenly Valley to Squaw Valley's bunny slope to the forested cross-country trails at Bear Valley and Kirkwood Meadows.

Its proximity to the Sierras and the sunny weather it enjoys for eight months out of the year make Sacramento a sportsman's paradise.

But recreational nirvana isn't restricted to teeth-clenching competitions, professional or amateur team sports, or strapping on skis, either snow or water. For many Sacramentans, it's as simple an act as summer barbecues in the park or a break from work with a noontime pickup game on a basketball court. It's a Sunday drive down the Delta to watch the sun set behind Mount Diablo. It's an afternoon's lull at one of the many new downtown cafes. It's a family outing to Goethe Park's Effie Yeaw Nature Center or William Land Park's Fairy-tale Town or the upgraded Sacramento Zoo also located there. But the one local recreational mecca that magnetizes nearly all Sacramentans to it sooner or later is the California State Fair.

Facing page: This hand-carved decorative horse is part of a recently added carousel at the state fair. Photo by Tom Myers

Right and below: From bodybuilding contests to livestock competitions, the attractions are diverse at the California State Fair. Photos by Mark Gibson (right) and Tom Myers

The State Fair: A Resurgent Tradition

"Meet me at the Golden Bear!" The assignation place needed no further description for Sacramentans from 1909 through 1967. It referred to the twin, lifesize golden bears who guarded the County Building, the main exhibition hall when the fair was located at Broadway and Stockton Boulevard.

From 1858 on, Sacramento has hosted the fair. And attendance was a ritual, an end-of-summer rite for Sacramentans, who took great pride in the annual event. There was livestock judging, the colorful displays in the County Building whose prizes when awarded carried year-long bragging rights, the wine competition whose gold medals conferred such prestige, and the furious race to the betting windows

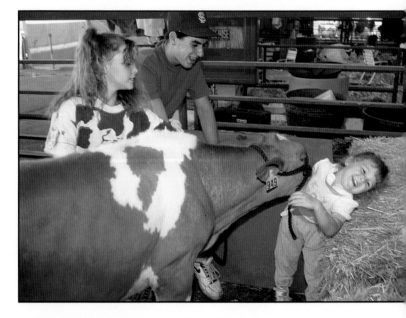

at the oldest horse-racing meet in the west.

The 10-day, mid-August to Labor Day run was unquestionably the most anticipated event of the year for Sacramento, and other than the capitol was the main source that differentiated it from other cities in the state. When you thought of Sacramento, you thought of the fair. When you thought of the fair, you thought Sacramento. The two were inextricably linked.

But when the fair moved from the overcrowded and aged facility to its present site along the American River parkway in 1967, the flavor didn't transfer with it. The old fairgrounds, shady and intimate and filled to capacity nearly every day, were displaced by a concrete and asphalt jungle whose discomfort was only exceeded by its placelessness. Architecturally cold and uninviting, the fair entered a long period of uncer-

tainty and poor management, resulting in low crowd turnouts and huge budget deficits. Frustrated with the fair management's ever-spiraling requests for state bailouts, in 1985 the legislature commissioned a study to consider the unthinkable: moving the fair out of Sacramento to a site at Fresno, San Diego, or Los Angeles.

When Joe Barkett came on board the rudderless ship as the fair's interim general manager in 1985, his first job was to prepare an assessment of what it would cost to shut down the Cal Expo site. Somehow, Barkett managed to convince a skeptical legislature to give him one more shot at righting the course.

Barkett described it as a three-pronged approach: "First, we promised to stick to our budget and come up with realistic revenue projections we could meet. The next thing we did was make fundamental, programmatic changes in the fair. We upgraded the landscaping, created more shady areas, started major new exhibits like Alice in Flowerland, and started doing nightly fireworks displays. The third prong was that we increased business during our non-fair time. That," continues Barkett, "was something that Cal Expos had never done very well in the past."

When enacted, the triad resulted in a bottom line that beat a $2-million deficit into a $4-million surplus by creating an environment that was inviting year-round.

The state fair is again, well, the state fair. The crowds, frozen in attendance at 550,000 for the five years prior to Barkett's arrival, now number over 750,000 annually, a number that has risen every year since 1985. Music from a half-dozen stages—everything from Dixieland to country to blues to rock'n'roll—floats through the sultry air. A new live-stock building, a Japanese Pavilion, and a brand new carou-sel have recently been added to the setting that is becoming as parklike as the old fair once was.

Now guarding the main parking lot entrance, the golden bears aren't precisely the meeting place that they were at the old state fair. Instead, they symbolize the continuity and perseverance of the capital city of a state that was once the Bear Flag Republic. A city that once struggled with its identity, altered and reshaped it, and now nurtures its future carefully.

Sacramento's Enterprises

Blossoming trees arch toward the sky in this photo of an almond orchard. Sacramento almond production out-strips other crops, and nuts processed in Sacramento are shipped to 94 countries around the world. Photo by Bob Rowan/Progressive Image Photography

CHAPTER 7

Networks

Sacramento's role as a modern, thriving metropolitan center is made possible by its network of communication, transportation, and energy providers.

Photo by Bob Rowan/Progressive Image Photography

AMERICAN AIRLINES

Early on the morning of April 15, 1926, a young aviator named Charles A. Lindbergh stowed a bag of mail in his little DH-4 biplane and took off from Chicago for St. Louis. Later that day, he and two other pilots flew three planeloads of mail from St. Louis to Chicago. Those trips were the first regularly scheduled flights for what was to become American Airlines.

At the time Lindbergh was chief pilot for Robertson Aircraft Corporation of Missouri, organized in 1921

American Airlines is the largest carrier in the free world.

and holder of the second airmail contract the government awarded to private operators under the Kelly Mail Act of 1925. Robertson was one of scores of companies that eventually became American Airlines.

Today American Airlines is the second-largest carrier in the world and the largest in the free world. It currently boasts a fleet of 565 aircraft and has orders and options to

purchase 248 more.

American Airline's relationship with Sacramento began in 1980, when it offered two flights to the hub city of Dallas/Fort Worth. Today the airline serves 210 cities worldwide with convenient connections from Sacramento Metropolitan Airport. Its international destinations include Europe, Latin America, the Caribbean, the Orient, the South Pacific, Canada, and Mexico.

Beginning with that first freight flight by a man who would become a

historic pilot, American has enjoyed a history of many industry firsts. Although dependent on airmail during its early years, American Airlines realized that the future of air transport lay in the development of passenger business. As early as 1934 it introduced the Air Travel Plan, one of the industry's first sales-promotion tools.

Breakthroughs in aircraft development ranked high among important innovations of the mid-1930s. American bought a few DC-2s that were good airplanes but still did not satisfy the industry's need for aircraft that could make money by carrying passengers. American's engineers decided that if they could increase the DC-2's capacity from 14 to 21 seats, the company would have an economical airplane.

The changes that were required turned out to be far more extensive than expected, and when the Douglas Company and American finished, they had a new airplane—the DC-3, destined to become one of the most famous commercial airplanes in history. American inaugurated commercial flights with the DC-3 between Chicago and New York on June 25, 1936. The DC-3, along with American's aggressive salesmanship, put the airline on a profitable basis. By the end of the decade American was the nation's number-one domestic air carrier.

In 1953 American pioneered nonstop transcontinental service in both directions across the United States with the DC-7. In January 1959 American introduced the Lock-

Above: American Airlines currently boasts a fleet of 565 aircraft.

Right: American serves 210 worldwide destinations with nonstop and connecting flights from Sacramento Metropolitan Airport.

heed Electra, the first U.S.-designed turboprop airplane.

On January 25, 1959, the company began the first cross-country jet service using the new Boeing 707s. American's first-generation 707 jets shortly became second-generation jets with the introduction of the turbofan engine, another industry first for American. The first fan-engine 707 went into service on March 12, 1961. In March 1962 American introduced Convair 990s, also powered by fanjets.

By mid-1988 the fleet numbered 452 aircraft, including two Boeing 747-SPs (for the Dallas-Fort Worth/ Tokyo route), DC-10s, Boeing 767-300 series and 200 series, Airbus 300-600s, B-727s, Super 80s, and a few B-737s and Baes obtained in the AirCal merger. Early in 1988 the airline placed an order for up to 100 B-757s.

Throughout the 1980s and now into the 1990s, American Airlines has prospered under the creative leadership of Robert L. Crandall. He was elected president and chief operating officer in 1980, and following the 1985 retirement of Albert V. Casey took on the additional titles of chairman and chief executive.

Crandall is credited with propelling the carrier through a turbulent decade of deregulation to the top of the heap. American today, according to a recent *U.S. News &*

World Report article, "is the biggest and best of the major U.S. airlines—an innovative and highly profitable carrier that even delivers good service."

George James, president of Airline Economics, Inc., a Washington, D.C., consulting firm, says, "American is the strongest of all; it's the best-managed airline in the world." Crandall's American invented crucial concepts that drove it and other carriers to dominance. American's Frequent-flier clubs' AAdvantage built customer loyalty; and computerized reservation systems drew travel-agent business and Super Saver discount fares.

By 1982 these and other service features earned American the distinction of being selected number one for domestic service in an International Airline Passengers Association survey for the fourth time. More than 14,000 of the IAPA's members (all are frequent flyers) took part in the survey. American has finished first in every poll ever taken by the association.

In 1988 American was named the best U.S. airline for the seventh consecutive year in a reader poll by the London-based *Executive Travel Magazine.* And that year, those readers named American Airlines the best transatlantic airline for the first time.

KFBK/Y92

KFBK Newsradio 1530 is where Sacramento hears the news first. As the Capital City's respected news leader, KFBK is the daily information source for thousands of Sacramentans and the voice of vital information and reassurance in times of emergency.

But KFBK is more than a source of news—it is the home of Sacramento's favorite radio personalities and the radio voice of the Sacramento Kings basketball team.

KFBK's roots go deep into Sacramento's proud and colorful past. On February 2, 1922, KFBK signed on the air as the very first station in the Sacramento Valley. Through the years, KFBK has played a leading role in many major community events, including the very first Sacramento Kings game, the Sacramento Dixieland Jubilee, the Fourth of July Fireworks Show at Cal Expo, and the California State Fair.

"Perhaps nothing exemplifies KFBK's commitment to excellence and community service more than the station's response to the 1987 San Francisco Bay Area earthquake," says vice president/general manager Rick Eytcheson.

KFBK traffic pilot "Commander" Bill Eveland was the first radio reporter in Sacramento to broadcast news of the disaster, and KFBK had the largest radio news team on the scene. Within 48 hours of the disaster, KFBK published and distributed an earthquake-safety brochure to its listeners. And KFBK listeners donated more than $38,000 to the Red Cross Earthquake Relief Fund.

KFBK is the station Sacramento businesspeople have come to depend on for reliable, frequent commuter traffic updates. It is the only Sacramento radio station with two airborne traffic reporters, Bill Eveland and Joe Miano, plus updates during the midday hours.

Traffic reports, plus an award-winning news team, weather from two certified meteorologists, stock market updates, play-by-play broadcast of the Sacramento Kings, and a crew of lively, intriguing, and per-

sonable news and talk hosts make KFBK Newsradio 1530 a vital element of the Sacramento scene.

Sharing and guiding KFBK's dedication to quality is the station's parent company, Group W Radio, Westinghouse Broadcasting Company. Like KFBK, its roots go deep as the nation's first commercially licensed radio station. Today Group W Radio is one of the largest and most-esteemed broadcast companies in America. KFBK Newsradio 1530 shares the pride of Sacramento from the Roaring Twenties into the twenty-first century.

As Sacramento's "Today's Hits, Yesterday's Favorites" station, Y92 offers listeners a blend of today's contemporary artists like Phil Collins, Anita Baker, Richard Marx, Huey Lewis and the News, Hall & Oates, and the Doobie Brothers. Each song is market tested among people in Y92's target demographic and lifestyle group for familiarity and likability, and the station reflects the city's prosperity, vitality, and booming growth. The music is hip, bright, and contemporary, yet the approach is clearly designed with adults in mind.

"What we play is the cream of the crop," says Y92 operations manager Jeff Sattler. "It's an exciting, contemporary combination and the most appealing sound for Sacramento's 25- to 44-year-olds."

Fast becoming Sacramento's favorite listen-at-work station, Sattler says, "We own the franchise of the 'No Repeat Workday,' meaning we never play the same song twice between 9 a.m. and 5 p.m."

Of special interest to the Sacramento business community is the quality audience Y92 delivers. Whether the advertiser is interested in the profound emergence of the woman working outside the home, or the impact of Sacramento's thousands of new residents, or the influence of the market's many upscale professionals, Y92 reaches affluent adults with active life-styles.

Commitment to the community is an important part of Y92's past and

present and is represented by yearly involvement with groups such as the Big Brothers/Big Sisters, American Cancer Society, Sacramento Food Bank, Multiple Sclerosis Society, and public television.

One of the most important services Y92 offers to Sacramento's business and professional community is airborne traffic reports. And in the Capital City, airborne traffic reports mean just one thing— "Commander" Bill Eveland. Y92 is the only FM station in the Sacramento market to possess this valuable commodity.

Y92 signed on the air in 1947 as Sacramento's very first FM station. It now broadcasts 50,000 watts from a tower in Elverta reaching listeners from Concord to Nevada City, and from Colusa to Jackson.

Behind Y92 is one of the nation's most respected broadcasting groups, Group W Radio, Westinghouse Broadcasting Company. The nation's first commercially licensed broadcast company now owns 20 radio stations in 13 markets.

Y92—along with sister station KFBK—is part of an esteemed broadcast tradition and a proud participant in Sacramento's rich past and bright future.

Facing page: When Sacramentans think of traffic, they naturally think of "Commander" Bill Eveland. Bill broadcasts traffic reports during morning and afternoon commute hours on KFBK and Y92 from "Newsflight One." KFBK offers more traffic reports than any other Sacramento radio station, and Y92 is the only FM station broadcasting commuter updates from the air.

GTEL

In the early 1980s the Federal Communications Commission and the California Public Utilities Commission delivered a one-two blow to the comfortable status quo of the telecommunications business:

—The FCC ordered a historic split between the telecommunications equipment business and the telecommunications service business; the marketing of equipment was deregulated and thrown open to competition, while providing transmission service continued under regulated, government-granted monopolies.

—The California PUC followed up the FCC order by telling GTE California—which was in both businesses—that if it wished to remain a marketer of equipment, it would have to form a completely separate subsidiary to do it.

GTE California had no intention of abandoning the customers who for decades had depended on the company for *all* their telecommunications needs. It accepted the challenge of creating a subsidiary with the creativity, aggressiveness, and quick reflexes demanded by a wide-open market—and in 1985 GTE California launched GTEL, a wholly owned subsidiary.

GTEL was a curious mix of regal corporate pedigree and venture capitalist feistiness—and still is. The customer premises equipment (CPE) market is the telephone business' Bermuda Triangle—a lot of companies enter it and disappear—but five years after its inception, GTEL is not only surviving, but prospering.

The secret of GTEL's success is that it refuses to be intimidated—by *anything*. It has consistently tackled projects that seemed too big and ideas that seemed too new. And flying in the face of conventional wisdom has paid off handsomely.

The most illustrative, most dramatic and most lucrative example of this trait: the vast telecommunications network GTEL is building for the state of California—CALNET. The only American public institution larger than the state government of

CALNET—California's communication network for 1991 and beyond.

California is the federal government, and the state's telecommunications and information management needs were commensurate with the scope of its operations.

GTEL was unruffled by the challenge. It conceived a statewide network that would vastly upgrade quality and the range of available services, and save money while it was doing it. It put together an all star team of subcontractors—IBM, MCI, Northern Telecom, GTE Telecomm. It staged a spectacular, real-life demonstration of CALNET's potential that wowed state experts. It faced down the competition, including a court challenge.

The result: a state-of-the-art, cost effective new network for the state of California—and another improbable but undeniable win for GTEL.

And CALNET is merely one very visible example of a long list of high-wire walks.

Such as:

—Reinventing the concept of the GTE Phone Mart—GTE's national, 120-location retail chain for CPE—by creating the "Multi-Mart," an innovative approach to serving both residential and small business cus-

GTEL has continually embraced the newest technologies and the biggest projects. The company has provided products and services for the county of Sacramento (Right) and the U.C. Davis Medical Center (Above).

tomers in the same state.

—Leading the rest of the telecommunications industry into the "electronic funds transfer" business—ATMs. ATMs were generally regarded as a financial business until GTEL planners took a second—and predictably convention-shattering—look and saw that they were computers wired to data bases and each other. That, they realized, is a telecommunication business—and GTEL leaped in.

At GTEL, however, death-defying feats of entrepreneurship don't overshadow a more venerable GTE value: a fierce commitment to customer

service. While GTEL's sales force is confounding the competition, its highly trained, highly experienced technicians—average tenure in the business: 15 years—are making sure that everything works as promised.

An uneasy combination of gleeful adventurousness and salt-of-the-earth conservatism? Absolutely. GTEL wouldn't have it any other way.

And neither would five years' worth of satisfied customers.

PACIFIC GAS & ELECTRIC

California had a population of less than 100,000 when the company that eventually became Pacific Gas and Electric Company (PG&E) was envisioned. Over the years the state grew to become the nation's largest—and a tiny gas company developed into the world's largest energy utility. The growth of each helped drive the growth of the other: California and PG&E have truly been partners in progress.

On a sunny day in 1850 two men stood on a sand hill contemplating a sprawling young San Francisco. Finally, one said to the other, "This is going to be a great city at no distant day. There will have to be gasworks and waterworks here, and whoever has faith enough to embark in either of these enterprises will make money."

The speaker had that faith.

Peter Donahue dreamed of a city where gas would light the dark streets and replace the oil lamps and can-

dles that dimly lit its dwellings and businesses. In 1852 he and a brother incorporated San Francisco Gas Company. It was the first gas utility in the West. And it was the ancestor of the great utility whose scope today would surely amaze even the farseeing Donahue.

In 1879 another enterprising utility pioneer saw new opportunities. That year a young San Franciscan named George Roe incorporated the California Electric Light Company in his city. It was the first electric company in the PG&E family tree—in fact, so far as is known, it was the first electric utility anywhere dedicated to public service.

Right: Hydroelectric power, generated by facilities such as the Pit 7 powerhouse in northeastern California, is one of the cleanest sources of electricity.

Below: PG&E's Diablo Canyon Nuclear Power Plant has won numerous awards for its performance.

In those early years local utilities were springing up everywhere. Soon a pattern developed: small pioneer gas companies merged with competitors, then merged with electric companies, consolidated into regional systems, and finally formed one integrated, interconnected system serving most of Northern and Central California.

Above: Natural gas is a clean, low-cost source of energy which over 3.2 million PG&E residential customers use to cook their food and heat their homes.

Left: Commercial energy audits and rebate programs can help customers use energy more efficiently and save money.

PG&E was incorporated in 1905. It united the successors to the companies of Donahue and Roe, and folded in pioneer hydroelectric power plants in the Sierra Nevada, many of them the work of two men whose names loom large in the PG&E story—Eugene de Sabla and John Martin.

They could not have been more unlike—de Sabla was a descendant of French nobility, and Martin was a self-made man, on his own since the age of 13. But they shared two vital qualities: vision and energy. Working separately and together, they built two hydroelectric plants, organized corporations, consolidated gas and electric systems, and created the sturdy foundation on which PG&E was built.

In the ensuing years PG&E has grown along with the area it serves, in turn providing energy to help that area grow.

PG&E and its predecessors helped the Central Valley to blossom. Promoting and providing electric power to irrigate its once-arid acres, they were a major force in creating one of the great agricultural areas of the world. By 1950, 98.5 percent of all farms in PG&E territory had electricity, far ahead of the rest of the nation.

The company met the demands of and helped to make possible the period of great growth after World War II that saw California pass all other states in population and become the nation's leading state by many measures. PG&E built powerful new generating plants to serve the new homes and industries, and extended its major gas mains to the state's northern and southeastern borders, there to tap supplies of natural gas from as far away as Texas and Alberta, Canada.

Throughout its colorful history, PG&E has never stopped pioneering. Spanning ever-greater distances with high-voltage power lines, it was able to develop more and more hydroelectric plants in the mountains. Today it operates the nation's largest investor-owned hydro system.

Harnessing natural steam from the earth, PG&E developed the first geothermal power plant in the nation. Expanding this resource over the years, the firm now operates the largest geothermal complex in the world.

Exploring the possibilities of the peaceful atom at government invitation, three decades ago PG&E was operating a nuclear power plant, which had been granted federal license No. 1. Building on this experience, the company's great Diablo Canyon Nuclear Power Plant, put in operation in 1985, has set records for performance.

Playing a lead role in developing alternative energy technologies, PG&E is project manager for a major nationwide research and development effort. Its aim is to raise photovoltaic generating units—which convert sunlight directly into electricity—to sizes economic for electric utilities. With all this, it is in character that PG&E should buy and deliver its customers nearly half of all the wind-generated electricity in the world.

PG&E has always changed with the times, and in just the past few years has been adapting to meet new, emerging needs in the energy-utility business. Residential customers remain reliant on the company, which in turn continues its commitment to serving them well. But because of partial deregulation and technological changes, larger customers increasingly have more choices: they can generate their own power or they can buy bulk quantities of natural gas from other suppliers and pay PG&E only to deliver it. Under chairman and chief executive officer Richard A. Clarke, PG&E itself is responding vigorously.

Streamlining its operations, cutting costs, and vigorously marketing its services, PG&E is changing—and staying the same. As it has been since the dawn of the century, PG&E expects to remain a partner in progress with the golden area it is privileged to serve.

MCI COMMUNICATIONS CORPORATION

It was said that it couldn't be done—that no one could break into the long-distance business and buck the monopoly set by AT&T. But in 1968 someone did, and 20 years later MCI Communications, known as the first company to create competition in the long-distance market, has advanced to become the second-largest telecommunications company in the world.

Barely into its third decade, MCI has become a global leader in providing a full array of voice, electronic mail, facsimile, and other products and services to business and residential communities.

With its growth, MCI established a presence in Sacramento, the fastest-developing region in the United States. In the 1990s the company is expanding further and locating a network management and customer service center in the greater Sacramento area.

The Sacramento expansion parallels the unprecedented growth that MCI has experienced both domestically and internationally. The company's Western Division, headquartered in San Francisco, includes 13 western states.

MCI's presence in the Sacramento area includes offices downtown as well as a billing center in Rancho Cordova. The center was established in 1983, and generates all of the company's billing and invoice transactions in 23 western states.

As it enters the 1990s MCI is placing an additional 550 jobs in the Sacramento area. The company has relocated its customer service center from San Francisco to Sacramento's Natomas Corporate Center, where the department occupies four floors and 85,000 square feet of leased office space.

MCI has purchased property in West Sacramento, where it is building an advanced network management facility that will monitor all of

MCI provides a full range of worldwide telecommunications services to millions of business and residential customers, state and federal governments, and other organizations.

the company's network functions in states west of the Mississippi.

MCI's Western Division president, Barry Wagar, describes the center as being a reflection of the billion-dollar commitment MCI has made to network expansion. "The new West Sacramento facility will further enhance the effectiveness and efficiency of our network," he says, "and we are very pleased to have it here in Northern California."

MCI competes internationally to provide a full range of global telecommunications services to businesses and residences, including long-distance telephone, fax broadcast, and electronic mail service.

"We have 50 major offices in 44 overseas countries," says Wagar. "Ours is a global business, and we are very encouraged by the number of companies here that do business internationally. With this global presence, it's no wonder that MCI and Sacramento are such a good fit."

MCI's sales branch and information offices are located at 8880 Cal Center Drive, Suite 150.

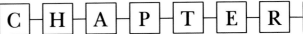

Professions

Sacramento's professional community brings a wealth of ability and insight to the area.

GREVE, CLIFFORD, DIEPENBROCK & PARAS

The law firm of Greve, Clifford, Diepenbrock & Paras is one of the area's most respected law firms. With a history dating back to the nineteenth century, the firm has continued to keep pace with the needs of its clients. Its more than 50 attorneys rank Greve, Clifford, Diepenbrock & Paras among the top five firms in Northern California in terms of size.

Greve, Clifford, Diepenbrock &

Senior partner Ed Clifford (left) with managing partner Larry Wengel.

Paras is headquartered in Sacramento, within blocks of California's capitol building and state offices. It also has offices in San Francisco and Chico to better meet the needs of the clients it serves.

A large part of Greve, Clifford, Diepenbrock & Paras' practice history was and continues to be cen-

tered around insurance defense litigation. The firm does substantial legal work for The Hartford, Aetna, Great American, Progressive, Safeco, The Home, Transamerica, Travelers, USF&G, Allstate, and State Farm.

The firm counts among its partners some of the state's most outstanding attorneys in the fields of insurance defense litigation, estate planning, tax, administrative law, and business litigation.

Sacramento offices of Greve, Clifford, Diepenbrock & Paras.

The firm represents a solid base of business, corporate, and individual clients including Union Pacific Railroad, Sears Roebuck, American Standard, Inc., Sacramento Savings, Sacramento County Employees Retirement System, Dean Witter, John F. Otto, Inc., Continental Heller Construction, Winncrest Homes, the California-Nevada Superspeed Train Commission, and numerous state and local agencies.

The firm is expert in professional malpractice defense and has represented attorneys, doctors, accountants, architects, bankers, engineers, realtors, and insurance agents and brokers in litigations and in front of such agencies as the California State Bar, the California Society of Accountants, the Board of Medical Quality Assurance, the Engineers Certification Board and the California Association of Realtors.

In construction law and real es-

tate, the firm represents owners, developers, contractors, engineers, and architects in all phases of their projects including land use planning, zoning, acquisitions, financing, property disputes, unfair compensation, torts, toxic tort liability, and commercial landlord/tenant matters. Today many commercial and real estate transactions are structured with an eye toward tax implications. The firms's practice embraces all aspects of tax advice and tax litigation.

In banking and consumer finance law, the firm handles litigation and regulatory problems of consumers, banks, savings and loans associations, and state and federal regulation of

GREVE CLIFFORD DIEPENBROCK & PARAS

consumer credit transactions. The firm also represents individuals, businesses, and financial institutions in both reorganizations and liquidations pursued in bankruptcy court.

Greve, Clifford, Diepenbrock & Paras is involved in all phases of its clients' business: forming new entities, trade secret protection, negotiating and drafting agreements and notes, negotiating acquisitions, sales and merger agreements, and rendering advice on specific transactions, labor and contractual disputes and employer-employee relations.

The firm assists its corporate clients in forming and structuring new corporations, mergers and acquisitions, preparing confidential private placement memoranda and registration statements for the issuance and offering of stock, preparing subscriptions and buy/sell agreements, and properly formalizing corporate activities.

Public affairs and governmental law is a rapidly growing area of Greve, Clifford, Diepenbrock & Paras' practice. It has legislative advocates in California, Nevada, and Hawaii.

The firm's extensive work with civil litigation, administrative law, and trial practice includes trial and appellate work at all state and federal levels, from the California Superior Court to the United States Supreme Court.

Greve, Clifford, Diepenbrock & Paras firmly believes that thorough preparation is the key to obtaining favorable results. It is the job of every attorney to keep his or her clients out of court if possible, but if litigation is necessary, Greve, Clifford, Diepenbrock & Paras is without equal.

KRONICK, MOSKOVITZ, TIEDEMANN & GIRARD

Since it was established in 1959, Kronick, Moskovitz, Tiedemann & Girard has developed a solid reputation in its representation of clients in matters involving water and natural resource law, education, legislation, public agencies, business, and litigation.

By providing responsive, cost effective legal services to deal with the immediate and long-range needs of its clients, the firm ranks among the top law firms in its areas of expertise. The firm bases much of its success on the teamwork of its individual attorneys collaborating their efforts to provide the most comprehensive services to deal with increasingly sophisticated legal problems. This sharing of knowledge and expertise among attorneys, coupled with the support from highly trained legal assistants and state-of-the-art research equipment, provides the foundation on which the firm operates.

Aggressive advocacy and preventative legal counseling are important components of the firm's legal services. The quality of services is re-

Above: (From left) Lloyd Hinkelman, Frederick G. Girard, Stanley W. Kronick, Adolph Moskovitz, and Edward J. Tiedemann. Photo by Quantum Studios

Below: (From left) Charles A. Barrett, Edward J. Tiedemann, and Janet K. Goldsmith. Barrett is of counsel with the firm, practicing primarily in the business department. Tiedemann practices in the public agency and resources department. Goldsmith is chair of the public agency and resources department. Photo by Quantum Studios

flected in its knowledge, expertise, and written capabilities which offer a depth of experience that is unique in the community of Sacramento law firms.

LEGISLATIVE
The legislative department of the firm offers complete representation for clients on legislative matters. Members of the firm are registered legislative advocates with the State of California, and appear regularly on behalf of clients before legislative committees and administrative agencies on a wide range of matters, including the adoption or amendment of statutes and regulations. The department's attorneys also appear before local legislative bodies such as the county boards of supervisors, city councils, and special district boards of directors to advance the interests of firm clients.

RESOURCES
The firm maintains an extensive natural resource practice. The expertise of the firm's attorneys include issues involving water rights, water quality, pollution, and contamination problems. The resources department provides sound legal counsel on the expanding area of environmental law, including hazardous waste and toxic substances, federal reclamation law, hydroelectric power financing and development, natural gas, and mining concerns.

EDUCATION
The education department represents more than 60 school and community college districts throughout California, as well as the California School Boards Association. The firm's attorneys provide legal counseling and representation in all areas of education law, including student issues, personnel, collective bargaining representation and nego-

William A. Kershaw (left) is chair of the litigation department. Michael A. Grob practices in the litigation department and is president of the firm. Photo by Quantum Studios

partment provide the full reach of transactional services involving contract drafting and preparation, negotiations, construction financing, documentation, and commercial transactions. Its services extend to governmental regulation/relations and international transactions with special emphasis on Pacific Rim countries.

LITIGATION

The firm's litigation department handles actions pending throughout California as well as federal courts and administrative agencies. The expertise of the department's attorneys covers not only controversies at the trial court level but also matters reaching both state and appellate courts. The diversity of the firm's experience extends from commercial, construction, and products liability matters to personal injury, medical malpractice, and insurance claims. The firm maintains a full service probate and bankruptcy practice at all levels, providing its clients with sound legal counsel on matters special to those legal areas.

Kronick, Moskovitz, Tiedemann & Girard maintains its commitment to the professional and business communities. The firm's attorneys actively participate in the state and local bar associations and contribute their energies to the advancement of legal education.

The firm has also made a substantial investment in the local community by devoting efforts to civic organizations, the arts, and a variety of charitable organizations. Its community activities were publicly recognized when the firm was the first recipient of the Sacramento Bar Association's special "Pro Bono" award for providing legal services to those in need without charge.

tiations from the management perspective, school finance, school construction planning and financing, governing board legal issues, and property matters.

PUBLIC AGENCIES

The firm provides legal services to more than 50 public agencies and municipalities, including among its clients many cities, counties, and school districts. The firm is able to provide effective legal counsel to virtually every aspect of concern to public agencies. Its services to water districts and water agencies, public utility districts, sanitary districts, recreation districts, fire protection districts, special assessment districts, and joint powers authorities have positioned the firm as an effective advocate to the unique aspects of public agency law, including land use planning, eminent domain, construction contract preparation, and

administration and federal reclamation law.

The firm's public agency attorneys provide legal assistance in the area of public finance. Their expertise includes bond financing, grant and loan application preparation, taxation, rate and charge setting, and public agency litigation matters.

BUSINESS

The business department provides a broad range of legal services to business clients. The department is designed to maximize effectiveness by structuring services to address the various stages of a business' evolution. Offering full services from the business formation stage, the firm counsels new and ongoing businesses on all aspects of financing, banking, tax planning, secured and unsecured commercial transactions, labor, and employment relations.

Other sections in the business de-

WRAITH & ASSOCIATES, INC.

Lawrence E. Wraith started with an idea in 1917 that the growing population and business sector of Yolo County needed a personalized approach to meet its insurance needs. Today, that same idea is the foundation of both Wraith offices, located in Woodland and Sacramento.

For nearly 75 years Wraith & Associates have served the insurance needs of agriculture, small business, and professional liability in Yolo County and since 1975 in Sacramento County as well.

"Many of our farming clients have been with us since the twenties and thirties," says Ronald D. Blickle, president of the firm and manager of the Sacramento office. "Where service is only a buzzword at many insurance agencies, it is the main ingredient in our successful relationship with long-standing clients. Service has been a cornerstone of Wraith & Associates since 1917."

Lawrence E. Wraith established his insurance service at a desk in the office of Garrette and Gill, Grain

(From left) A.B. Allen, owner of Allen Transportation Company, with Ron Blickle, president, and Bill Miller, vice president of Wraith & Associates, Inc., have been doing business together since 1947. Photo by Jeff Burkholder/Life Images

(From left) Dave Cunningham, vice president; Ron Blickle, president; Bob Giannoni, vice president; and Bill Miller, vice president. Photo by Jeff Burkholder/Life Images

Brokers, located in Woodland. The grain brokerage was a bustling place in those days as the agriculture industry brought Yolo County into the twentieth century. When he wasn't behind his desk, Lawrence Wraith could be found visiting people in their stores, on their farms, and in their homes.

The personalized insurance service that Wraith envisioned had become a reality in Yolo County. Business continued to grow during the post-World War II era and Caswell D. Swett joined Wraith in 1951, leading to the establishment of Wraith & Associates.

The commerce in Yolo County continued to boom as products were shipped outward. The county seat of Woodland also became a thriving service community. As the community grew, so did Wraith & Associates. Richard C. Lunt became the third partner in 1959, joined 10 years later by Elwood H. Blickle. The four friends ended the partnership in 1972 and es-

tablished a corporation—Wraith & Associates, Inc.

Wraith & Associates, Inc., expanded their geographical coverage in 1975 by purchasing the insurance business of Charles R. Cusack in Sacramento, but continued to operate the Sacramento office under the Cusack name. In 1981 the Sacramento operation was moved to larger offices and the name was changed to Wraith & Associates, Inc., once again uniting the personalized insurance service under one name.

In May 1990 *The Sacramento Business Journal* ranked Wraith & Associates, Inc., the seventh-largest property and casualty insurance agency in the Sacramento area.

"Today that commitment to personalized service remains with our staff of licensed professionals," says Blickle, who was elected president of the firm in 1988.

The current owners of the firm, in addition to Ron Blickle, are David Cunningham, vice president of life, accident, and health; Bob Giannoni, vice president of sales; and Bill Miller, vice president of marketing. The vibrant, young management team looks forward to continuing a tradition of growth through serving the insurance needs of their diverse list of clients.

(From left) Bob Eoff and Fred Heidrick, Jr., owners of Heidrick Farms, Inc., with Dave Cunningham and Bob Giannoni, vice presidents of Wraith & Associates, Inc. Photo by Jeff Burkholder/Life Images

Photo by Richard Kaylin

The Marketplace

Sacramento's retail establishments and accommodations are enjoyed by residents and visitors alike.

Photo by Ed Asmus Photography

WILLIAM GLEN

"There's nothing like this in Boston!" "There's nothing like this in New York!" "There's nothing like this in San Francisco!" These comments are frequently heard as visitors from all parts of the world discover William Glen. William Glen is more than just a store, it is an experience of abundance. Any attempt to define William Glen is too limiting.

Founded in 1963 by William (Bill) Snyder and Glen Forbes, in 1978 William Glen became the anchor store of Town & Country Village when they moved to the 11,000-square-foot central building in that shopping center. Both California natives, the owners of William Glen could see that Sacramento was craving a source for sophisticated and refined tableware and serveware. Determined to accomplish this, William Glen established relationships with every major manufacturer of fine china, crystal, and flatware in the world to offer Sacramento the design they required. With more than

Right: In celebration of William Glen's 25th anniversary, the partners unveiled a new 12-shops-in-one shop.

Below: Glen Forbes (left) and William Snyder believe the key to success is customer service. Photo by Jensen Photography

1,000 china patterns and 600 patterns of crystal and fine flatware, William Glen was presented the top Design Award by the Gifts & Decorative Accessories judging panel for innovative store design in 1989, and in 1991 was nominated by the tabletop industry as the premier tabletop specialty store on the Pacific Coast.

Today William Glen, with 30,000 square feet, embraces the abundance of gracious living. Not only will customers find the widest selection of tableware, but also the smell of fresh coffee beans roasted daily on location—as well as fragrant potpourri, soaps, and bath oils. Crisp table linens ranging from the refined and elegant to bold and colorful abound, along with brilliant lead crystal bowls and vases, candles and

oil lamps, small innovative electric appliances, books on every culinary subject, a broad selection of the finest cookware made, an arsenal of cutlery, fine bakeware, and every conceivable gadget for food preparation and decoration.

During the recent remodeling in 1989, the William Glen Market was incorporated into the store design with a fine assortment of packaged specialty gourmet foods and wines, as well as an extremely popular salad, sandwich, and dessert cafe where customers may pause for some refreshment while shopping or linger leisurely over cappuccino, expresso, or a glass of wine.

Silk flowers and artificial plants and trees, as well as garden accessories and unique bird houses are displayed on the "main street" aisle with storefronts inviting you to visit the many departments that make up the store. Among the prestigious lines you will find represented in the crystal department are Baccarat, Orrefors, Lalique, Waterford, and Kosta Boda. In fine china admire Lenox, Cartier, Wedgwood, Fitz & Floyd, Noritake, Christian Dior, and Ralph Lauren. Among the collectibles are David Winter, Duncan Royale, Swarovski, and Lladro. Silver flatware and holloware is represented by Gorham, Christophle, Lundt, Kirk Steiff, and Towle. William Glen has an extensive Bridal Registry, and provides educational demonstrations to local organizations emphasizing new directions in tabletop design.

Now established as one of Sacramento's leading business citizens, William Glen cooperates with many Sacramento organizations to enhance the quality of life in the community. Working with the Sacramento History Center, the Sacramento Medical Auxiliary, Sacramento Junior League, and the Jesuit Loyola Guild, William Glen has been recognized as a major contributor to Sacramento activities.

TOWN & COUNTRY

Brick-paved patios and ivy-covered walkways bursting with colorful seasonal flowers invite the discerning customer to Town & Country Village—a landmark shopping center just seven minutes north of Downtown Sacramento. Established more than 45 years ago on the northern rural edge of the growing capital city, Town & Country Village was the first suburban retail center to be built west of the Mississippi—a concept so successful that it was soon replicated in cities throughout the western United States.

Specialty shops, restaurants, and services make up the unique open air center that is Town & Country Village. Architecturally, it is a blend of early and contemporary California with red tile roofs meeting wisteria-covered treillage to provide cool, shaded sidewalks.

More than 60 specialty shops and restaurants offer today's sophisticated consumer the ultimate in dining and shopping, encompassed in an atmosphere that is both elegant and relaxed.

Nationally acclaimed William Glen is a "shop like no other." The extraordinary tabletop shop features china, crystal, kitchenware, and gourmet foods. Fine men's clothing with European styling and contemporary flair can be found at Bonney & Gordon. Patrick James, clothier to men and women who prefer traditional styling, incorporates an elegant Talbott tie shop as well as a men's shoe salon where the finest in men's footwear can be found. DeMilles and Ransohoff's, long-time favorites of discerning fashion-conscious woman, feature clothing and accessories ranging from casual to elegant. At Elyse you'll find European and American designers in elegant surroundings. Brentano's bookstore invites shoppers to come in and browse amidst the finest of-

Above: The highly acclaimed Caffe Donatello features classical Tuscan cuisine in an elegant and warm atmosphere.

Left: The Town & Country Village is made up of a unique assortment of specialty shops, services, and restaurants.

ferings in print. The village has two fine florist specializing in artful floral design. Stylish boutiques and specialty shops featuring personally fitted lingerie, high-fashion shoes, bridal fashions, athletic footwear, and accessories cater to women of all ages.

No matter what your appetite, Town & Country Village has something to tempt the palate. The highly acclaimed Caffe Donatello features Chef Greg Neville's classic Tuscan cuisine in an environment as visually stunning as the food. Compadres offers platters of fresh and spicy authentic Border cuisine. Elsewhere, foods range from continental to a French-style creperie, and a sweet tooth can be satisfied

with handmade chocolates, gelato, ice cream, and the best doughnuts in town.

The Village is frequently the locale for philanthropic events, some that have become community traditions. Whatever special items a person might need, from clothing or food to toys and travel, Town & Country has a long-established tradition of offering the finest in the capital region.

The Village is designed with a blend of early and contemporary California architecture, with red tile roofs meeting ivy-covered treillage to provide cool, shaded sidewalks.

HYATT REGENCY SACRAMENTO AT CAPITOL PARK

Long before its doors first opened on April 6, 1988, the Hyatt Regency Sacramento had already established itself as the capital region's can-do hotel. Through its first two years as a member of the downtown community, it has continued to play an active role.

The fact that it exists at all is an odds maker's nightmare. The grand opening festivities, filmed by "Good Morning America," followed nearly 15 years of frustration for a dozen or more luckless developers who tried and failed to construct a luxury hotel on the corner of 12th and L streets. Sacramento developer Bob Cook, a partner in the hotel building (the land is owned by the city), once dubbed the project "heartbreak hotel." It took the combined troubleshooting skills of local real estate heavyweights Joseph Benvenuti and Gregg Lukenbill to bring the project to completion.

But that is all prologue. Today, in the capable hands of general manager Gunter Stannius, the Hyatt Regency Sacramento has taken on both the glamour and the responsibility of the city's only four-diamond downtown hotel.

Mediterranean in architectural design, with arched windows and marble floors, the hotel features $500,000 in (mostly locally produced) commissioned artwork and European antiques. Its prime location, directly across the street from the California State Capitol and immediately adjacent to the Sacramento Community Theatre and Convention Center, attest to the willingness of city officials to hold out as long as they did for a first-class facility.

Meeting a long-standing desire for first-class downtown Sacramento accommodations, the Hyatt offers 502 deluxe guest rooms, 62 Regency Club rooms (10th floor), and two private Gold-Passport floors (the fifth and the nonsmoking ninth). Nonsmoking floors for registered guests are the sixth and seventh. There are 14 handicapped-equipped

Left: The entrance to Bugatti's is adorned with iron grillwork designed by Sacramento artist Michael Riegel.

Below: Located in downtown Sacramento, the Hyatt Regency is directly across the street from the state capitol and adjacent to the Sacramento Community Theatre and Convention Center.

rooms on the third and ninth floors. All rooms are spacious and feature individual climate control, color television, direct-dial telephones, and many include a balcony and spectacular views of the Capitol and the Sacramento Valley. Regency Club accommodations include complimentary continental breakfast, personal concierge service, guest robes, morning newspaper delivery, evening hors d'oeuvres, and good night cordials.

The hotel features 30 luxury suites, including the Governor's Suite (14th floor) and the Grand Terrace Suite (12th floor). Both of these popular suites offer tremendous views of the capitol and Capitol Park, as well as grand pianos and in-room whirlpool baths.

A large free-form swimming pool surrounded by lush landscaping is available for hotel guest use as well as a first-class health facility featuring up-to-date workout equipment. A full gift shop including toiletry items is located in the hotel lobby and a convenient shopping arcade is located within the hotel. Same-day valet service and shoe shines are also available. A 632-car covered garage

Spacious rooms offer generous living areas, beautiful furnishings, and modern amenities.

offers parking to hotel guests and visitors.

The Hyatt's two restaurants and three lounges offer something to the liking of a wide variety of tastes. Bugatti's, the 190-seat, three-meal restaurant, features indoor dining and patio dining next to the fountain. Serving a full section of Mediterranean favorites and classic Italian cuisine, Bugatti's opens for American fare breakfast at 6 a.m. daily. Bugatti's is open until 11 p.m. nightly, and midnight on Friday and Saturday. A champagne brunch is served every Sunday.

The atmosphere of Dawson's, a 90-seat chophouse, resembles that of a private club, while the menu features steaks, chops, and fresh fish grilled in a display kitchen. Chilled prawns and several varieties of fresh shellfish are offered at Dawson's Raw Bar.

Named after the classic Arabian

The atmosphere of Dawson's, a 90-seat chophouse and bar, resembles that of a private club.

stallion, Amourath 1819, the lobby bar features live piano music nightly and poolside seating. On the 15th floor, Busby Berkeley's offers panoramic views of the Sacramento skyline and entertainment Tuesday through Saturday nights.

But perhaps most importantly, the Hyatt provides much needed downtown meeting space to go along with its first-class hotel accommodations. The facility offers more than 27,000 square feet of specially appointed meeting and banquet space including the Regency Ballroom with 15,544 square feet of freestanding hall and seating for up to 1,800 people. The ballroom has six subdivisions and, in addition, the hotel offers 12 conveniently located rooms that accommodate from 10 to 200 people. With the ability to facilitate meetings from 10 to 1,800 people, the Hyatt has quickly become a fa-

vorite event and convention site both locally and statewide.

In addition to working closely with the Sacramento Convention and Visitors Bureau to draw state and national conferences and conventions, the Hyatt has also aligned itself with area cultural arts and charity groups. In June 1988 the weekend-long Gala for the Arts held at the Hyatt Regency grossed more than one million dollars for the Sacramento Regional Foundation. According to Sacramento cultural art officials, this represented the most money raised for the arts in Sacramento during a single event.

Working with the arts and charity groups comes with the territory, according to general manager Stannius.

"The cultural community is very important to us. At Hyatt we feel it is our responsibility to support a variety of cultural activities whenever possible. As part of the Sacramento community, we feel compelled to give back a portion of what we receive, and we feel that all businesses have a moral obligation to react in kind."

As noted earlier, the hotel is home to a large collection of locally produced artworks. The gates and grill-work at the entrance to Bugatti's as well as all banisters and the second

floor guardrail is a commissioned piece by Sacramento resident Michael Riegel. In designing the gates and railings, Riegel focused on imagery that symbolizes the state of California, and more specifically, the city of Sacramento—the oak tree, Sacramento River, the sun, and the poppy. The Hyatt collection also features nine wall pieces by Leslie Toms, a mural (in Bugatti's) by Stephanie Taylor, and 10 oil paintings by Fredric Dynan Dalkey. All three artists are Sacramento natives.

In addition to participating in Sacramento events, the Hyatt brought to

The Capitol Boardroom and Regency Ballroom's 27,000 square feet of meeting space enables the Hyatt Regency to facilitate meetings of from 10 to 2000 people.

the area the corporation's annual World's Largest Office Party. In December 1988 the Hyatt introduced the popular holiday event to more than 900 enthusiastic party goers and raised more than $5,000 in the process. Money raised went toward the construction of Camp Ronald McDonald, a children's charity. Each year, throughout the world, Hyatt Regency's designate local charities as recipients of the holiday event.

Playing an active role in the local arts and charitable service scene is not the only responsibility Stannius and the Hyatt have had to shoulder.

"Being a first-class downtown hotel has also meant leading the way by example," says Stannius. "The Hyatt project is part of the catalyst needed to get other projects going in the redeveloping downtown area. It is hoped by us and others that the success of the Hyatt will help bring about needed expansion of the convention center."

"Once the center is expanded, larger groups will come to town which will bring more hotel proj-

ects to the area," notes Stannius. "It's a chain reaction that will inevitably bring more money to the city's coffers."

While a majority of the Hyatt's business is currently made up from conventioneers, Stannius and city officials would like to see tourist business further developed.

"With the noted exception of the annual Dixieland Jazz Festival held over Memorial Day weekend, Sacramento's tourism industry is in its infancy," says Stannius. "But with Old Sacramento, the railroad museum, and the renovation of the state capitol, the future looks bright for the Hyatt and Sacramento."

And with its downtown location, the Hyatt will be in good position to reap the benefits of an improved

tourism market. Historic Old Sacramento is only eight blocks away and in addition to featuring more than 200 shops and restaurants is also home to the highly acclaimed California State Railroad Museum. The governor's mansion is just five blocks away. Outside the back entrance is the quickly developing K Street Mall, which offers some of the area's finest retail outlets. The hotel is located only three miles from Cal Expo, site of the California State Fair and Waterworld Amusement Park. It is 15 minutes from the Sacramento Metropolitan Airport, 90 minutes from downtown San Francisco, and two hours to South Lake Tahoe.

"We're well positioned for Sacramento's future," says Stannius. "And from my perspective, it looks great."

Below: Amourath 1819, the lobby lounge which was named after the world-famous race horse, features live piano music nightly.

RED LION HOTELS & INNS

Anyone who visits Sacramento either decides to make it a permanent stop or leaves with unforgettable memories of the city's unique and captivating charm. The picturesque Sacramento Valley retains its rural mystique even with an abundance of affluent businesses, state government offices, and a growing and sophisticated urban population. Sacramento remains a frequent stop for both the business and pleasure traveler.

The Red Lion Hotel of Sacramento and the Sacramento Inn, a sister hotel, exemplify these characteristics. Located just off Business 80, the two beautifully landscaped facilities epitomize Red Lion's philosophy of catering to its guests. Even though hundreds of people walk through its doors every day, Red Lion believes each individual guest should feel as though they are the most important person in the hotel. Customer service is always first priority, providing both comfort and security.

As guests arrive at the beautiful Red Lion Hotel, the custom-designed western architecture provides a sense of comfort and hospitality. The 448 relaxing and luxurious rooms offer amenities, including attractive furnishings, air conditioning, color television, direct-dial phones, and king- and queen-size beds. In addition, two elite presidential suites and nine parlour suites cater to executive entertainment or special occasions.

In Maxi's Dining Room guests are treated to a repertoire of exquisite dishes that are showcased with distinctive presentation and finesse. The delightful, casual setting of the Coffee Garden offers breakfast, lunch, and dinner, with everything from Belgian waffle breakfasts to prime rib dinners.

For casual entertainment, Maxi's Lounge boasts vintage wines and refreshing cocktails in a comfortable

Above: The Red Lion Hotel's custom-designed western architecture provides guests with a sense of comfort and hospitality.

Left: The Sacramento Inn offers 14 conference and meeting rooms, including this elegant ballroom.

setting. Live entertainment and dancing are enjoyed throughout the week.

With more than 30,000 square feet of flexible meeting space, including 17 banquet rooms, the Red Lion Hotel can help plan a business meeting for large and small groups ranging from 10 to 1,500 people. Every function is efficiently and professionally handled.

Just across Arden Way is Red Lion's Sacramento Inn, featuring 378 relaxing guest rooms with air conditioning, color televisions, direct-dial phones, desks, and king-, queen-, or full-size beds. Five elegantly furnished deluxe suites, each with its own full bar and invigorating Jacuzzi, are also available.

An extensive renovation in 1990 has transformed the Sacramento Inn's dining room into a new, uptown restaurant. The expanded restaurant, with its pastel colors and relaxing atmosphere, will offer a

delectable menu featuring a variety of pasta, seafood, beef, and poultry dishes in addition to a refreshing salad bar.

The Sacramento Inn also offers 14 conference rooms designed for flexibility and comfort. Combined with that of the Red Lion Hotel, the two locations provide nearly 45,000 square feet of space, an amount that can accommodate almost any event.

Both the Red Lion Hotel and Red Lion's Sacramento Inn are within walking distance of various movie theaters, restaurants, and nightclubs, as well as Cal Expo, the site of the California State Fair, and Arden Fair, the largest shopping center in the region. Guests can also visit the State Capitol Building, the governor's mansion, Old Sacramento, Sutter's Fort, the State Railroad Museum, Crocker Art Museum, and the Sacramento Zoo, all within a ten-minute drive. San Francisco, Lake Tahoe, and the Napa/Sonoma wine country can be reached by car within two hours.

Whether visitors are in the city for business or pleasure, the Red Lion Hotel and the Sacramento Inn can make their trip a memorable one.

FRANK FAT, INC.

In 1939 Frank Fat bought a defunct Italian restaurant and created a California legend: Frank Fat's. A culinary dynasty was born, one that for more than 50 years has reflected Frank's belief in hard work, extraordinary food, and service above and beyond the call of duty.

Today, at their three restaurants in Sacramento—California Fat's, Fat City, and Frank Fat's—the Fat family continues to experiment with new dishes and flavors, improved cooking techniques, and innovative design, much to the approval of their customers, both old and new.

Throughout Frank Fat's life, the common denominator has been food. As a child in China, he was part of a family that owned a wine and rice business. On immigrating to America his early jobs included picking fruit, waiting tables, and dishwashing. Now, at more than 85 years of age, he is Sacramento's premier restaurateur, the patriarch and driving force of the Fat family.

Because of the downtown location of his 50-plus-year-old Frank Fat's restaurant, and the glowing reputation it earned as the place to go to do legislative business over the years, Fat has become a prominent figure in the Chinese community, and a man counted as friend and equal to the most prestigious names in California politics.

Though Fat has known every governor for the past 30 years, he remembers one in particular. When Governor Earl Warren became Chief Justice of the United States, he invited Frank into his chambers. For a Chinese immigrant with no political pull, the event was "the highest honor" of his life.

His son, Wing, says the invitation came only "because he's Frank Fat and because he has always been courteous to those who have lunch

Frank Fat's interior blends a traditional Asian motif with unconventional colors, style, and materials, courtesy of renowned designer Anthony Machado.

or dinner in his restaurant."

In 1984 Frank Fat decided to refurbish the little restaurant where politicians dined. The price of the job was rumored to be $1.3 million. When it reopened on Fat's 80th birthday, two blocks of L Street had to be roped off to accommodate 8,000 invitees, thousands of whom showed up in tuxedos and evening gowns. Assembly Speaker Willie Brown presented a resolution praising Fat. Sacramento Mayor Ann Rudin proclaimed "Frank Fat Day."

The master of ceremonies was U.S. District Court Judge Thomas MacBride. "My most reliable sources tell me that the cost of restoring this restaurant was $8 less than it cost to redo the Capitol," MacBride said at the time.

Today Frank Fat's at 806 L Street is a standing legend. The menu offers classic regional Chinese dishes, choice cuts of aged steak, and Frank's famous banana cream pie. The interior blends traditional Asian motifs with avant-garde colors, style, and materials.

Frank Fat, owner.

Fat City, at 1001 Front Street in Old Sacramento, is a turn-of-the-century French cafe/saloon, complete with stained glass, Tiffany lamps, and a polished, 100-year-old mahogany bar trimmed in brass. The menu features light appetizers, hearty lunch and dinner entrees, and rich desserts.

The newest restaurant of the trio is California Fat's at 1015 Front Street in Old Sacramento. Designer Anthony Machado's innovative decor, built around a spectacular 30-foot waterfall, is a feast for any set of eyes. Executive chef Lina Fat's menu combines California basics with the great flavors of the Pacific and Asia.

Frank Fat's, one of the state's great restaurants, offers classic Chinese dishes, choice cuts of aged steak, and Frank's famous banana cream pie.

TENCO

For the past 60 years Northern Californians have turned to Tenco Tractor, Inc., for high quality farm and construction equipment. A firm proud of its colorful and successful past, the Caterpillar equipment dealer looks to the future with excitement and optimism.

The company has grown from a small tractor shop in Marysville to a $100-million dealership whose 10 facilities serve a vast 34-county territory in Northern California. Tenco now sells and services equipment for a broad range of industries, including logging, site construction and heavy construction, paving and compacting, landleveling, power generation, trucking, industrial material handling, and agriculture.

"We are rightfully proud of the

Two Caterpillar D10 tractors, in tandem, push a 651 wheel scraper at Peter Kiewit Pacific Division, Rocky Ridge Roseville.

company my grandfather started in the midst of the Depression," says Gordon K. Beatie, president and chief executive officer of Tenco. "Tenco has survived and succeeded because of its ability to be progressive and innovative, and to aggressively change with the times."

Indeed, Beatie's grandfather, Daniel W. Beatie, had set the pace for progress when he risked all he owned to found Marysville Tractor and Equipment in 1931. Having grown up on a farm, he knew first-hand the struggle for survival. He later worked on a railroad, then moved into banking. With a strong combination of hard work and business knowledge, Beatie built a business that not only survived the Depression, but emerged a solid and successful

Caterpillar dealership that continues to grow.

By 1969 the business encompassed ten counties (hence the renaming of Marysville Tractor and Equipment to Tenco Tractor, Inc.) and was growing so rapidly that Dan's son Ken, who by then was company pres-

The Caterpillar engine model 3512, which is installed at City of Sacramento, Pocket Road Sub Station.

each to help a deserving student continue to a four-year university.

"We need to be actively involved in the regional educational process in order to ensure an adequate employee base for our company," says Beatie. "For instance, there just are not enough heavy equipment diesel mechanics being trained locally, so we decided to take matters into our own hands."

Towards this end, Tenco has been working closely with Delta College in San Joaquin County to develop a new training facility that offers students hands-on experience in addition to the classroom learning. "Skilled labor is a vital and rare resource these days," says Beatie, "and helping to provide this resource is good for the community and good for us."

Tenco looks forward to Northern California's projected growth, which will augment an already active market base far into the future. In order to support and service these new markets, Tenco plans to expand their already diverse and extensive product lines and inventories.

In addition to equipment sales and service, Tenco offers rentals and leases, plus a parts inventory worth more than $8 million. Customer service is Tenco's highest priority. With more than 150,000 square feet of state-of-the-art facilities, including a large fleet of field service vehicles and factory-trained technicians, Tenco meets their customers' needs with prompt, efficient service.

Says Gordon Beatie, "As Northern California continues to grow, Tenco is committed to meeting increasing customer needs with the best possible equipment and service. Tenco readily accepts this challenge as we work toward another 60 years of total commitment to customer satisfaction."

Top: Caterpillar agricultural tractor, Challenger 65, works at Scheidel Ranch in Sutter County.

Bottom: A Caterpillar lift truck model V80E works at Berco Redwood in Sacramento.

ident, moved the corporate headquarters to a 160-acre site in South Sutter County near the Sacramento Metropolitan Airport.

Today Tenco is devoting its resources not only to its own growth, but also to its surrounding communities. In the past seven years Tenco has become more community oriented than ever, according to Gordon Beatie. His father, Ken, has been actively involved with community organizations including the Boy Scouts, and his brother, Dan, (who also heads Tenco's Power Division) manages the family-owned Donner Mine camp in Yuba Gap which accommodates nonprofit organizations. Currently, Tenco contributes to numerous community organizations and causes, the most significant of which is its annual scholarships program. Nine regional community colleges receive $1,500

CHAPTER 10

Finance

Sacramento's solid financial base has provided a dynamic environment for the economic growth and opportunity of both individuals and businesses in the community.

Photo by Bob Rowan/Progressive Image Photography

SUNRISE BANK OF CALIFORNIA

In the late 1970s Citrus Heights was recognized as one of the fastest growing communities in the Capital City region. To serve this growth at a local level a group of 40 area business leaders founded Sunrise Bank of California on October 13, 1981. Sunrise Bancorp was incorporated on November 20, 1981. Two subsidiaries were formed under the holding company—Sunrise Bank of California and Western Sunrise Mortgage Corporation.

Steven P. Thomas, chairman of the board, says "Sunrise Bank is a firm believer in giving back to our community what our community has so generously given to us."

He says the bank's products and services have benefited the Citrus Heights, Rancho Cordova, and Roseville communities by providing jobs and employment opportunities for residents and by filling the need for an independent, local bank in the area.

"All decisions are made on a local level," explains Thomas. "Our management is accessible and involved in the community."

Sunrise Bank's commitment to customer service is quickly apparent as one walks in the door of any of its three locations. Sit-down teller windows are provided so that customers can conduct their banking business in a private, relaxed setting.

"Our management team has an open door policy," notes Thomas. "We encourage our customers to call on us for personal assistance at any time."

Sunrise Bank products are designed to meet the needs of its customer base—the real estate construction industry and the business and professional market. The bank's real estate lending group serves as a premier interim lender by providing creative financing and consultation to the region's major builders and developers as well as the community at large. A major focus of the bank, according to Thomas, is to serve the construction financing needs of the home builder addressing the upscale housing market ($250,000 and above).

Business lending at Sunrise Bank is personalized by a team of highly qualified lending professionals who have the insight and expertise to offer the right financing program for its clients' needs.

"We get to know our clients and their businesses through office visits, facility tours, and comprehensive analysis of financial data," says Thomas.

Sunrise Bank offers many creative financing programs such as lines of credit, including inventory and receivable financing; terms loans; and equipment financing. In 1990 the bank introduced home equity lines of credit. Sunrise Bank also serves the needs of small businesses as a lender under the SBA (Small Business Administration) program. In addition, the bank provides many types of consumer loans that assist in major purchases, home improvements, personal lines of credit, and premium Visa gold credit cards.

In September 1989 Sunrise Bancorp, the parent company of Sunrise Bank of California, received approval from the NASDAQ National Market System Committee to have its common stock listed on the NASDAQ national market system. Shareholders, customers, and investors are now able to check the activity of the bank's stock and receive consistent quotations via the listings in the major financial publications as well as most major newspapers.

Sunrise Bank also conducts a quarterly series of free community-service seminars. These informative programs serve as a thank you to existing customers and as an attraction to prospective customers. One seminar featured a panel discussion on three critical areas of business success: legal, insurance, and financial areas. Another seminar was held on the advantages of wills and living trusts.

Besides being a friendly independent bank, Sunrise Bank also wants to offer its customer the best in technology through its state-of-the-art data processing system. In 1988 the bank converted to a new data processing system that through its flexibility and comprehensiveness has enhanced overall customer service and allowed the bank to provide customers with products and services not previously available.

"Virtually all information concerning a customer is on-line now, which enables us to provide immediate response to customer account inquiries," says Thomas. "Notices and statements have been designed to provide more descriptive and detailed account information for easier customer reconciliation. The system has been planned to take Sunrise Bank well into the future."

Sunrise Bank of California is well positioned for growth with three choice branch locations. The landmark headquarters building in Roseville houses the bank's administrative offices, the real estate department, and the Roseville branch operations. The Rancho Cordova office is ideally located in the midst of a flurry of new office parks, hotels, motels, and restaurant developments. The Citrus Heights office was relocated to a more convenient location

A primary focus of Sunrise Bank is serving the financing needs of builders of upscale homes.

in 1989. This site offers improved access, parking, and visibility within the community that comprises Sacramento's largest suburb.

A subsidiary of Sunrise Bancorp, Western Sunrise Mortgage Corporation is a full-service mortgage banker. It combines a local retail operation with a statewide correspondent network offering a wide variety of residential loan products.

In August 1988 Western Sunrise Mortgage Corporation assumed the operations of the mortgage banking division of Sunrise Bank. Operating as a separate subsidiary of Sunrise Bancorp provides the ability to expand geographically, as well as generate greater loan volume by the use of outside warehouse lines of credit as a source of funds. During 1989

Western Sunrise funded $200 million in residential mortgages—an 80 percent increase over 1988 production.

On the wholesale side, Western Sunrise Mortgage Corporation has cultivated a network of correspondents made up of mortgage brokers, mortgage bankers, banks, and thrifts. More than 80 of these retail lenders throughout Northern California and Nevada funnel loan packages to Western Sunrise for underwriting, document preparation, and funding. In 1989 a correspondent loan purchasing program was initiated. The program has proven to be exceptionally successful, as it now accounts for 25 percent of total loan volume. Near the end of 1989 Western Sunrise also instituted an expansion into the Southern California market that will further enhance the company's position in the industry.

WELLS FARGO BANK

Wells Fargo Bank has been a partner in Sacramento's growth since 1852—longer than any other California bank. From the boomtown days of the gold rush to the city's current growth and expansion, Wells Fargo has stood for reliable, quality service.

With more than 40 branch offices in the area, 100 automatic teller machines, more than 1,000 employees, and almost $2 billion in deposits, Wells Fargo ranks among the largest retail banking outfits in Sacramento. And Wells Fargo is without equal in the agricultural lending arena, qualifying as the leading commercial-bank agricultural lender in the region as well as the United States. In fact, Wells Fargo's commitment to agriculture started in the early 1850s and has remained constant through good times and bad.

From the beginning the bank's hallmark traits, as stated by Henry Wells himself, were integrity, reliability, flexibility, and dedication to hard work. These values were important to the banking public of the 1850s and remain popular with today's consumers and businesses.

"Wells, Fargo & Co. is now ready to undertake a general Express Forwarding Agency and Commission Business and the purchase and sale of Gold Dust, Bullion, and Specie." With this simple announcement, Wells Fargo's Sacramento agency opened its doors at 45 Second Street in July 1852, beginning a long tradition of service to the Sacramento community that continues today. During the Gold Rush Sacramento was a busy river town and the jumping off point for those seeking their fortunes in the Mother Lode. Many who set out for such gold country diggings as Gouge Eye, Poker Flats, Murderer's Bar, and Poverty Hill returned to Sacramento with great fortune. Others returned only with dashed hopes. These were hard times.

Wells Fargo's early years in Sacramento were not easy. In November 1852 a disastrous fire swept through the fledgling city, destroying most of its business district, including the Wells Fargo office. The bank's headquarters in San Francisco were quick to respond with the first of many corporate contributions to Sacramento. Because more than 1,600 buildings were burned down, Wells sent relief money to the sufferers of the fire.

One month after the fire a levee on the American River burst, flooding the city. Two weeks later, just as the December floodwater was subsiding, the Sacramento River overflowed its banks, once again inundating the city with water.

Despite these setbacks Wells Fargo continued to provide dependable banking and express services to the young community. In many respects the office's first agent, Isaac Hubbard, was responsible for Wells Fargo's prosperity amid such adverse conditions. Not only was Hubbard an extremely able agent, he also was an important member of the Sacramento community. He served as the city's chief engineer and helped construct the network of levees and bridges that would prevent future flooding of the city.

Above: A Wells Fargo shipping tag, circa 1900. Courtesy, Wells Fargo Bank

Left: Wells Fargo's diamond-shaped sign signaled horse-drawn express wagons to stop for parcels and identified company offices worldwide. Courtesy, Wells Fargo Bank

Below: A Wells Fargo treasure box was often an outlaw's quest. J.Y. Ayer of San Francisco built them of Ponderosa pine and reinforced them with oak rims and iron straps and corners. The weighed 24 pounds, measured 20 by 12 by 10 inches, and rested in the front "boot" of a stagecoach beneath the driver's feet. Courtesy, Wells Fargo Bank

In January 1854 Wells Fargo moved to the newly constructed Hastings Building at the corner of Second and J streets. A local newspaper commented that Wells Fargo had "a very fine office containing all the modern improvements of a good and convenient express banking office." This is the same office restored to its original style that tourists to Old Sacramento can visit today.

This historical museum, known as the Wells Fargo's Old Sacramento

Agency, is located one block from the world famous Railroad Museum and is a prime example of the look of an Old West banking office. There one can step into the past and see the basic tools of the early banker's trade—gold scales, a clock, and a letter press. These simple tools, combined with energy and resourcefulness, helped Wells Fargo agents get the job done quickly and accurately.

The most prominent artifact on display is a magnificent copper and brass balance. The scales are very

Above: A Wells Fargo wagon banner, 1915. Courtesy, Wells Fargo Bank

Right: A page from Samuel Colville's 1854 Sacramento directory details the products and services Wells Fargo offered gold seekers far from home. Courtesy, Wells Fargo Bank

Below: Cisco, California, 1867: Wells Fargo's stagecoaches met the Central Pacific Railroad to begin a 1,500-mile journey to the Union Pacific railhead at North Platte (Morrow's Station), Nebraska. Courtesy, Wells Fargo Bank

rare; fewer than 100 were made originally. The primary use was to weigh gold dust and nuggets found in the mines of the Mother Lode. Each balance was meticulously made to exacting specifications, earning it a widespread reputation for dependability and accuracy. Miners, whose livelihood depended on an accurate assessment of their

This advertisement for Wells Fargo's Great Overland Mail Route, the most extensive stagecoaching network in the West, ran in the California Business Register in 1867. Courtesy, Wells Fargo Bank

gold, claimed that the scales could register the weight of a lead pencil mark on a sheet of paper.

Also on display is a nineteenth-century letter press. In the days before carbon paper, high-speed copiers, and facsimile machines, agents used this letter press to copy important documents.

Wells Fargo's technological advances continued into the twentieth century. As part of Wells Fargo's support of agriculture, it helped develop refrigerated railroad cars that made possible transport of Sacramento's agricultural products to markets in the East.

Recognizing the potential of the city's growth, in 1911 Wells Fargo established divisional headquarters in Sacramento and moved its offices to the Forum Building at the southwest corner of Ninth and K streets.

James L. Tucker supervised the company's activities during this time. A Wells Fargo agent since 1904, Tucker was also an active member of the chamber of commerce, various historical societies, and sat on nu-

merous parade and celebration committees. It was under Tucker's supervision that Wells Fargo's domestic express business became part of the government sponsored American Railway Express on July 1, 1918, in the midst of World War I.

One of Wells Fargo's strongest banking competitors, the American Trust Company, opened an office at Seventh and J streets in 1934. Four years later the office moved to 10th and J. In 1960 the American Trust Company merged with Wells Fargo, and the 10th and J office, with its historical decor, serves Wells Fargo Sacramento customers to this day.

During the California gold rush, Wells Fargo's expertise and integrity

in the gold business earned the company a reputation for being the most reliable and efficient banking and express company of the western frontier. Though that role has changed and grown since those early days, the high standards of service remain intact.

As an active member of the Sacramento community, Wells Fargo has continued its early commitment to the area's future. Out of that commitment Wells Fargo became one of a group of private sponsors who joined state and city governments in the Old Sacramento redevelopment project that began in the 1960s. As part of the restoration, Wells Fargo reopened its Old Sacramento Agency office and later converted that banking office into a history museum.

Wells Fargo's commitment to Sacramento extends to the city's cultural programs as well. As an avid supporter of the arts, Wells Fargo has sponsored performances of the Sacramento Ballet and enabled students of 20 local schools to experience the beauty of dance. Wells Fargo has also sponsored projects of the State Railroad Museum, the Sacramento Symphony, the California Historical Society, and the Crocker Art Museum, where works of art donated by the bank are on display.

Wells Fargo's Sacramento office, located in the B.F. Hastings Building from 1854 to 1857, was an important banking and gold dust buying center. Today it houses a Wells Fargo Bank history museum. Courtesy, Wells Fargo Bank

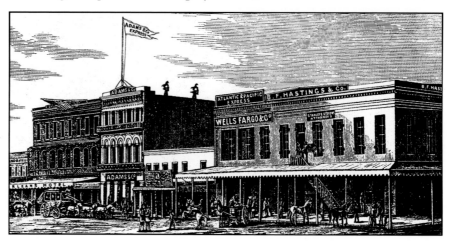

Wells also was a founding sponsor of the Sacramento Sesquicentennial, celebrating the city's 150 years.

But providing quality banking service to the Sacramento community continues to be Wells Fargo's main concern. Wells Fargo was the first major California bank to extend its banking hours during the week and to open on Saturday. In addition to longer banking hours, in 1988 Wells Fargo became the first bank to offer 24-hour, person-to-person phone service with every checking account. This innovative service allows customers to call a Wells Fargo Express Agent® day or night to verify a checking account balance, transfer funds between accounts, or stop payment on a check. For customers who prefer to do their banking at an ATM, Wells Fargo established a local network of 100 automated teller machines, with more than 1,300 throughout the state. And to extend customers' ATM access throughout the country, Wells Fargo joined the Star System® and nationwide PLUS® ATM system.

Wells Fargo also serves Sacramento's business community with an extensive range of products and services. In fact, Wells is a leading commercial lender in the area's middle market. Longtime local companies have relied on Wells Fargo to help finance their growth for the past 138 years. The bank's Real Estate Industries Group continues to fund some of the area's largest real estate development today. And Wells' regional commercial banking office specializes in high-tech products such as cash management and 401k retirement programs as well as highly personalized services such as commercial loans and asset management.

The Asset Management Division manages the wealth of more than 25,000 organizations and individuals statewide, including nearly $29 billion in personal assets for clients. Wells Fargo also handles $68 billion in pension-fund money—more than some banks many times their size. One of the reasons is that Wells pioneered the advanced portfolio management technique of systematic management of risk and return. These strategies have kept Wells among the top-performing money managers for the past dozen years. In addition, the division offers a wide variety of investment management products, from short-term liquidity management to long-term endowment and trust fund management. The division's strengths are complemented by the bank's other investment resources, such as the pension subsidiary, Wells Fargo Nikko Investment Advisors (the largest equity index manager in the nation), and the economics group, which enjoys a nationwide reputation for excellence.

As Sacramento grows so does Wells Fargo's investment in the area. Recently five new Wells Fargo branch offices opened in the region: Roseville, Cameron Park, Rocklin, Greenhaven, and Laguna Creek.

Plus Wells Fargo is constructing one of the tallest buildings in Sacramento complete with a new history museum, office space, restaurants, and retail stores. The building is scheduled for completion in early 1992. The 30-story Wells Fargo Center on Capitol Mall will house 500,000 square feet of office space, as well as the Bank's Sacramento Main Office. The new Wells Fargo History Museum will display an original Concord stagecoach, just like those that rolled across the western frontier carrying money, mail, and merchandise to California's early settlers.

The museum also will house an authentic Wells Fargo Agent's office from the gold rush and railroad eras, so children and adults alike can actively relive the Old West. Historical artifacts from Sacramento's important Chinese community will be on display, too. All this will be set among two murals with vistas of the Sierra Nevada and the Sacramento Valley surrounding the museum-goer. Large historical photographs of familiar Sacramento landmarks also will decorate this special museum.

Today, just as in the past, Wells Fargo is committed to the four values Henry Wells spelled out in the 1850s. The bank's sound and stable financial management is a sign of its commitment to integrity; reliability is apparent in Wells' guarantee of accuracy and thoroughness; flexibility is abundant in the bank's innovative products and responsiveness to the marketplace; and hard work is a necessary component for Wells Fargo to provide the high level of quality service its customers demand and have come to expect from the West's oldest bank.

Wells Fargo Bank is proud of its longtime commitment to Sacramento in the past, is excited by its present success, and is looking forward to a continuing partnership with the city in the future.

COMMERCE SECURITY BANK

Commerce Security Bank has been built with a clearly focused strategy in mind: to be the premier financial institution in all aspects of real estate.finance in the Sacramento region and to fund its operations by offering top rates and quality service to depositors.

"As this strategy itself is simple, the key to our success has been its execution," says Peter H. Paulsen, chairman of the board of the Sacramento-based financial institution. "In this respect, we distinguish ourselves with our people and our approach to customers."

REAL ESTATE DEVELOPMENT AND INVESTMENT
Experience, reliability, flexibility, and speed is what's required in to-

day's fast-moving and competitive real estate market. Commerce Security Bank prides itself in providing its customers with just that.

Commerce Security Bank has assembled a top team of experienced real estate professionals. All approvals, inspections, and funding take place locally so the decisions can be made with the speed and efficiency real estate development professionals require.

"Commerce Security Bank stands as a financial partner in every aspect of the real estate field, from lending to an individual for the construction of a custom home to financing an entire subdivision, shopping center, or industrial project," explains Grosvenor G. Nichols, Commerce Security Bank CEO. "We are also an

active partner in the development process through our joint venture activity which provides equity to builders for selected real estate projects."

HOUSING
Commerce Security Bank's leadership is made up of individuals whose careers have been built around real estate. Each residential home transaction receives individual attention from the date of application to the date of funding from a personal loan officer. The local bank combines the mortgage

The headquarters of Commerce Security Bank is located in the Point West area of Sacramento.

lending expertise of a large institution with the personal attention of a hometown bank.

To meet all its customers' needs, Commerce Security Bank offers a complete line of mortgage products, including FHA and VA loans, conventional fixed and adjustable rate mortgages, and jumbo mortgages, with a selection of options such as extra-quick qualification and fixed-rate conversion for ARM loans. Commerce Security Bank also offers owner/builder lot and construction loans.

SAVINGS AND PERSONAL INVESTMENTS

"Top rates and excellent service. That's what our customers demand and that is what we give them," says Nichols. "Our customers enjoy a friendly, personal banking environment, with no long lines or unreasonable paperwork demands. Yet our deposit accounts consistently pay among the highest interest rates in the area."

Commerce Security Bank offers its customers a complete spectrum of federally insured depository instruments, including passbook savings, certificates of deposit, regular and commercial checking, and SuperNOW and Money Market checking accounts. In addition, the local institution offers such services as Visa, bank-by-mail, safe deposit, night drop, cashier's checks, travelers checks, and courier service for business accounts.

"Because Commerce Security Bank is a local bank, committed to strengthening the Sacramento area, our customers are truly making a long term investment, benefiting from both the top interest rates they receive and the knowledge that their money is reinvested in the Sacramento community," says Nichols.

COMMUNITY PARTNER

As a locally owned and operated financial institution, the success of Commerce Security Bank depends on the success of the Sacramento region. Thus participation in the community is not only good citizenship but good business as well.

"As an institution, we invest our support in many of the organizations which are contributing to positive growth in this region," notes Nichols.

Commerce Security Bank serves as corporate sponsors of KVIE and the Sacramento Children's Receiving Home, and co-sponsored 1987's March On Baseball to help bring professional baseball to Sacramento.

In addition, Commerce Security Bank employees hold vital roles in such organizations as the Sacramento Valley Teen Challenge, the California Vietnam Veterans Memorial Commission, the Sacramento Chamber of Commerce, Sacramento Country Day School, the Sacramento Metropolitan Arts Commission, the Sacramento Ballet, and the El Dorado Sheriff Search & Rescue Team.

"We have an outstanding team of motivated managers and employees," says Nichols. "These people are our most important asset, and our corporate culture is to listen carefully to them, to be responsive to their needs, and to treat them with compassion and respect.

"We view our customers as our financial partners," continues the CEO. "Our partners in savings and personal investments, our partners in real estate development and investment, and our partners in housing."

The result of this high regard for employees and customers has been success for Commerce Security Bank: substantial market penetration in a short period of time and outstanding financial performance.

"As we enter the 1990s full of confidence, we remain committed to our real estate strategy, our people, our customers, and the long term prosperity of the Sacramento region," says Paulsen.

On May 15, 1991, Commerce Security converted from a savings and loan to a state bank charter. According to Paulsen, "this will enable us to diversify into commercial business banking, broadening the scope of the services we will offer to the Sacramento marketplace."

CAPITAL POWER FEDERAL CREDIT UNION

In April 1954 seven employees of the Sacramento Municipal Utility District decided that local financial institutions weren't in tune with their money needs—so they chartered their own.

Today the Capital Power Federal Credit Union has more than $20 million in assets, nearly 7,000 members, and just opened a high-tech headquarters office in East Sacramento. Despite this successful growth, Mary McPoil, president and general manager of Capital Power, says the credit union remains committed to its original mission statement:

"Capital Power Federal Credit Union will be responsive to members' financial needs by providing superior personal service in a cost-effective manner."

In a nutshell, McPoil says, "We're not bigger, just better at personally meeting the needs of our members."

In addition to the recent completion of the new headquarters building on Folsom Boulevard, Capital Power members can be proud of many other recent improvements:

"We expanded our ATM service with the addition of five networks throughout the country; we introduced TELLER LINE, our audio-response system providing home and office access to Credit Union services; we converted to a new data processing system; we enhanced savings programs by creating add-on Gold Certificates of Deposit, tiered-rate IRA accounts, and greater latitude in rates and terms on regular CDs; and we added an overdraft line of credit to our share draft checking programs," reports McPoil.

While these improvements were achieved, McPoil notes Capital Power maintained its financial stability. "The local credit union's well-being is measured by our growth in assets, member savings, outstanding loans, and additional reserves and

Above: Capital Power's new high-tech headquarters, located on Folsom Boulevard in East Sacramento, is a symbol of the company's growth and commitment to the community.

Left: Capital Power's beautiful new lobby is equipped with all the most modern amenities and services.

retained earnings," says McPoil. "Other measures of financial stability are, of course, the competitive rates we pay on all our regular shares, certificates of deposit, IRAs, and other savings programs and the low rates we charge for loans."

Capital Power has also recently gained special recognition for its efforts in bringing credit union services to family members. For this program, the local credit union was awarded the Family Marketing Award from the California Credit Union League. Capital Power was also the recipient of the California community achievement award which recognizes the credit union's involvement in community projects and activities.

Additionally, all members of the Capital Power board of directors re-

cently completed the prestigious and rigorous Volunteer Achievement Program, developed by the Credit Union National Association.

"Ours is the only credit union in Sacramento—perhaps the only one in the state—whose entire board has completed this demanding program," says McPoil. "The achievement is a clear demonstration of our board's commitment to the service of their fellow members."

Capital Power Federal Credit Union remains faithful to the credit union principle of "people helping people"; to that purpose, McPoil says it will continue to provide a full range of high-quality, low-cost services, and at the same time maintain the sound financial base vital to the cooperative.

"Our mission statement charges us to provide 'superior personal service in a cost-effective manner,' and we intend to hold to that purpose," McPoil emphasizes. "After all, member satisfaction is our business."

From the Ground Up

A thriving building industry provides the expertise to shape the Sacramento of tomorrow.

Photo by Bob Rowan/Progressive Image Photography

MALONEY AND BELL, GENERAL CONTRACTORS, INC.

Maloney and Bell's work on the Roseville Center, a free-standing retail space, highlights their attention to detail in all phases of construction.

It's nice to win awards. They're recognition of hard work and an affirmation of commitment to quality and excellence.

So when Robert A. Bell, president of Maloney and Bell General Contractors, Inc., learned that one of his firm's projects—the Cal Farm renovation—had been selected as office building of the year by Building Owners and Managers Association (BOMA) he was very pleased and proud.

"Contractors don't often enter their work in competitions. Most of us are so busy keeping up with our projects that we don't have time," notes the president and sole owner of the Rancho Cordova-based general construction firm. "In fact, we didn't enter our project in the BOMA competition—it was entered by Cal Farm Insurance."

This type of an award was a first for Bell and his 10-year-old firm (although the firm had earned "Best Renovation" honors for its work on Five Points Shopping Center in Carmichael). He didn't know what to think of this honor. Just how important is this sort of recognition? Does it just make you feel good or does it

lead to increased business? Those were just a couple of questions Bell found himself asking. In search of answers, he called a local architect in a prominent Sacramento architectural firm.

"They've won dozens of awards. I felt that if anyone would be able to determine the value of winning an award, they would," says Bell.

The architect's response? To Bell's surprise he downplayed the importance of awards.

"Awards help us compete for jobs, but they're by no means a big part of our marketing program," the architect explained. "To me, their greatest value is that they act as a yardstick to mark where we stand in the marketplace. Entering a competition forces you to define the problem, the problem-solving process, and the solution," continued the architect.

The lesson learned by Bell more than two years ago was that good work, more important than awards, is what keeps the customer happy.

"Awards? They're nice. But I'm

more pleased by the fact that Cal Farm thought enough of our work to enter the project in the competition. That's award enough for me," says Bell.

Maloney and Bell General Contractors, Inc., was chartered as a California corporation in November 1981 by Robert A. Bell and John H. Maloney. The corporation was restructured in 1986, with Bell assuming sole ownership of the company.

Through more than 10 years of work within the greater Sacramento capital region, the firm has achieved an outstanding reputation in all phases of commercial construction and renovations, including retail, industrial, office, fire- and earthquake-damaged structures, and tenant improvements.

"The firm negotiates and bids competitively for contracts on both new work and renovations," explains Bell.

Maloney and Bell, Inc., is well known among architects and clients for quality workmanship, timely completion of projects, and competitive pricing.

The renovation that Maloney and Bell performed for Cal Farm Insurance Company in Sacramento won them the office building of the year award from the Building Owners and Managers Association.

New York; Warren, New Jersey; and Philadelphia, Houston, Jacksonville, Cleveland, Detroit, and Pittsburgh.

Historically, McLaren/Hart prided itself in its ability to offer a full range of turnkey environmental services for problem definition, solution, and prevention. Through this focus McLaren/Hart has a proven track record of accomplishments, many setting precedents, which have established McLaren/Hart as a premier environmental consulting firm.

McLaren/Hart has worked on more than 1,000 waste sites, including a 10,000-acre aerospace facility where more than 500 monitoring wells were designed and constructed to investigate the occurrence and distribution of contaminants to depths up to 500 feet in a geologically complex, multilayered aquifer system.

The company has designed, installed, and operated a full range of contaminated soil and groundwater treatment systems. As the 1990s begin, McLaren/Hart-designed systems are treating 100 million gallons of groundwater daily. McLaren/Hart has remediated more than six million cubic yards of contaminated soil.

McLaren/Hart has assembled the nation's largest chemical risk assessment team—ChemRisk. The team is staffed by nationally recognized Ph.D. and master's degree-level health scientists and toxicologists. Successes include reducing remedial investigation costs at an Illinois site. Previous consultants suggested an $8-million investigation; the Chem-Risk assessment was completed for $2 million and resulted in saving the client additional millions of dollars in remediation costs by demonstrating as acceptable the "no action alternative" rather than the proposed major pesticide remediation. Extensive toxic tort/expert witness testimony has been provided by the firm. Technical expert witness support was provided for the first successful defense of toxic tort brought by private litigants claiming $100 million in dam-

McLaren/Hart's Asbestos Management Group provides an extensive team of professionals and technicians trained to provide asbestos abatement management oversight services.

ages for alleged well contamination.

The company has provided extensive turnkey underground tank management services—monitoring, removals, and installations. For one client alone, McLaren/Hart removed more than 100 tanks ranging in size from 150 gallons to 47,000 gallons, designed and installed 55 new double-walled underground tanks, and managed the associated soil remediation program.

The firm has conducted more than 2,000 property transaction environmental assessments, including a 178-site investigation in five states in five weeks. It also managed a seven-state assessment of 142 commercial and industrial properties involving 5,600 acres and 8.5 million square feet of facilities; the investigation resulted in securing a $400-million loan.

McLaren/Hart has developed an unparalleled bio-remediation team—BioR$_x$—staffed by multidisciplinary professionals who understand contaminated systems' complex physical, chemical, microbiological, and political parameters. BioR$_x$ has a history of successful site treatments from 700 to 250,000 cubic yards of contaminated soil.

McLaren/Hart's commitment

Sacramento's largest environmental engineering consulting company, McLaren/Hart, has its corporate headquarters in Rancho Cordova.

to its clients begins with its staff. "Through our reputation we have attracted an eminently qualified, highly trained staff of professionals encompassing the full range of environmental disciplines," explains McLaren. "Our staff is chosen for technical talents, quality education, dedication to their technical field, experience, and energy."

The multidisciplinary staff resources includes engineers, hydrogeologists, soil scientists, toxicologists, certified industrial hygienists, air-quality specialists, regulatory support staff, AHERA-certified asbestos inspectors and managers, health scientists, chemists, and computer specialists.

With this multidisciplinary staff, McLaren/Hart is able to offer the following services: remedial investigation and feasibility studies, chemical risk assessments, soil and groundwater contamination remediation, biological remediation, multipurpose modeling, underground tank management services, air resources management, property transaction environmental assessments, asbestos assessments, regulatory compliance and permitting support, hazardous materials management, applied industrial hygiene, environmental impact reports, an in-house hazardous materials analytical laboratory, soil vapor surveys, and geotechnical engineering.

3DI, INC.

In 1989, when the City of Sacramento selected 3DI, Inc., to provide project and construction management services for the adaptive reuse and renovation of Memorial Auditorium, it was an historic first for the city.

"3DI is the first construction management firm the City of Sacramento has hired for a major building project," says Chuck Kluenker, vice president for the international construction management services firm. "The Memorial Auditorium renovation is a major undertaking for the city. They needed assurances that the job will be done right, come in at cost, and be completed in a timely manner. We're here to help make sure that happens. The city can't afford any surprises."

3DI's responsibilities include architectural program evaluation, assistance with architectural selection, A/E design review, cost estimating, value engineering, scheduling, bid management, construction management, and transition planning. 3DI's

3DI has major commissions in other capital cities such as the Pentagon renovation in Washington, D.C.

3DI serves as project manager for the Sacramento Auditorium renovation project.

estimating group prepared a schematic design estimate. Along with the estimate, 3DI provided suggested cost savings that totaled $2.6 million in proposed schematic design budget and design adjustments. In collaboration with the city and the architect, $2.2 million of cost savings were accepted to maintain the original budget.

3DI is the largest subsidiary of 3D/International, Inc. As the firm's project management subsidiary, 3DI offers management services in capital construction markets including project, construction, maintenance, and pre-design management. The 3DI management team has provided services to public, commercial, and corporate clients on construction valued at more than $20 billion.

"Unlike other project and design construction management companies that have a standard approach to management, 3DI believes in retaining an open-ended flexible approach that can be tailored to our client's needs," notes Clifton E. Wright, 3DI chairman and CEO. "Despite our experience in providing the same services to countless

other facilities, we still view each assignment as unique and deserving our specialized attention."

3DI's strength lies in being able to fine tune and calibrate its multidisciplined expertise to the nuances and dynamics of every project the firm undertakes. Through its rigorous attention to detail—from project startup through completion—3DI has proven to corporate, academic, and institutional clients that their concerns and 3DI's are often one and the same.

"At 3DI, we speak the language of the architect, the engineer, the general contractor, and the regulator," says Wright. "Our versatility and responsive approach is particularly attractive to clients who seek better or novel ways to achieve their goals. It also offers owners greater representation, control, and accountability to their projects. Most importantly, it gives us the freedom to innovate and excel—to be the first ones our clients turn to when they need a fresh view of what has gone before."

CHAPTER 12

Quality of Life

Medical, educational, and service institutions contribute to the quality of life of Sacramento area residents.

Photo by Dick Schmidt, courtesy The Sacramento Bee

MERCY HEALTHCARE SACRAMENTO

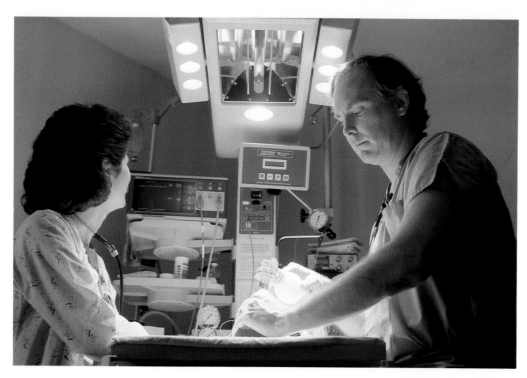

A special intensive care unit for newborns at Mercy San Juan Hospital helps premature infants to begin healthy lives.

The mission of the Mercy hospitals is inspired by the love of God; the example of Catherine McAuley, the founder of the Sisters of Mercy; and the Catholic heritage of healing and cherishing life. The fundamental element of the Mercy Healthcare mission and philosophy is "service to all in need." Mercy's philosophy statement articulates this concept: "We believe in the rights of all persons to quality health care and our responsibility to act as advocates for the poor and those with special needs."

The Sacramento area Mercy hospitals can trace their origins back to October 1857, when several Sisters of Mercy arrived to provide education and medical care to the gold miners and their families. Over the next 40 years the Sisters established several schools and orphanages and provided what would today be called "visiting nurse" services.

In 1896 the Sisters established the first private hospital in Sacramento. Known as "Mater Misericordiae" (Latin for "Mother of Mercy"), the hospital was located at 23rd and R streets. In 1925 this hospital was relocated to a new building at 40th and J streets and renamed Mercy General Hospital.

Today Mercy Healthcare Sacramento encompasses three area Mercy hospitals: Mercy General Hospital, Mercy San Juan Hospital, and Mercy Hospital of Folsom. Mercy Healthcare Sacramento, the corporate entity governing the three Sacramento Mercy hospitals, was formed in early 1987 following the creation of Catholic Healthcare West.

Known throughout Northern California for its tertiary cardiac services, Mercy General Hospital also provides a wide range of other specialized services. The entire hospital complex has just completed a major renovation project that has resulted in the creation of a "new hospital from within."

This 489-bed hospital offers general medical and surgical services, intensive care, and emergency services; cardiac surgery, cardiac catheterization, and cardiac telemetry; respiratory telemetry; orthopedics; oncology; obstetrics; pediatrics; acute rehabilitation; comprehensive outpatient services including outpatient

surgery, lithotripsy, laser center, and diagnostic imaging services (CT/MRI/radiology); and a continuing care center.

In 1967 the Sisters of Mercy responded to the growth of Sacramento's northern area with the establishment of Mercy San Juan Hospital, located in Carmichael. This 217-bed hospital is now undergoing major renovation to modernize its existing and new services to meet the challenge of the 1990s.

Mercy San Juan is located at 6501 Coyle Avenue. Its services include general medical and surgical services, intensive care, and emergency services; obstetrics and neonatal intensive care unit; cardiac catheterization; pediatrics; oncology; neurology; hyperbaric oxygen therapy; a sleep center; diagnostic imaging (CT/MRI/radiology); and comprehensive outpatient services.

In 1980 the Sisters of Mercy acquired Folsom's Twin Lakes Community Hospital. At that time they made a pledge to the Folsom community: to improve the existing facility, and ultimately to build a new hospital. Mercy fulfilled this pledge. Renovation efforts provided significant improvements to the existing facility, while the new hospital was being planned. In May 1989 the new hospital was unveiled to the community. Mercy Hospital of Folsom is now equipped to meet the current and future needs of the Folsom and foothill communities.

This new 95-bed facility has the capability to expand to 250 beds. The hospital will continue to focus on providing general medical and surgical care to serve the young families who will form the core of the area's population for years to come. Its location near the center of the Folsom community allows for conve-

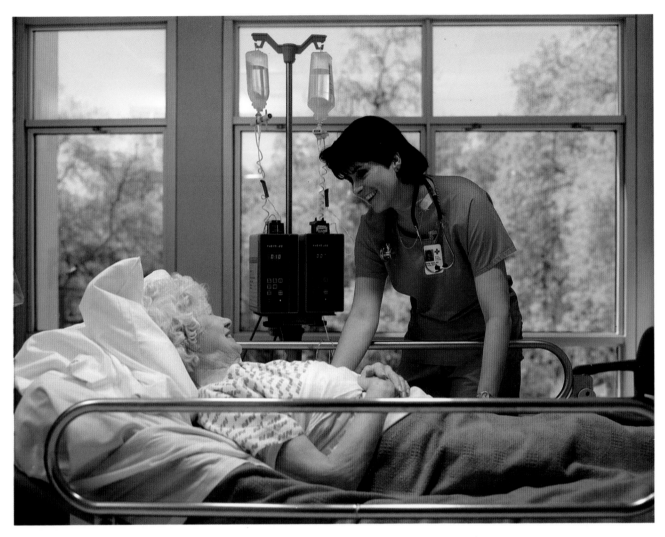

nient referrals of patients with serious medical needs to one of the two
other regional Mercy hospitals.

Services offered at Mercy Hospital of Folsom include general
medical services, intensive care, and
emergency services; obstetrics, pediatrics, and diagnostic imaging (CT/
mammography/radiology); and a
laboratory.

In today's era of rapid technological change, the hospitals are committed to continually offering the most
advanced and sophisticated services
to patients. In 1987 the Mercy hospitals were the first local hospitals
to provide kidney stone lithotripsy,
which provides a nonsurgical alternative to kidney stone removal. One
year later Mercy General Hospital led
the nation with the arrival of a gall
stone lithotripter, providing similar
relief to gallstone sufferers.

*Generations of Sacramento families have
come to rely on the Mercy hospitals to provide competent, compassionate care.*

Other major high-technology
services offered by the Mercy hospitals include the area's most advanced and comprehensive laser
center, hyperbaric oxygen therapy,
and a new medical program that
vastly increases the chances of recov-
ery from stroke.

Mercy is also concerned about
the need to provide information
and support to members of the community. The hospitals offer Ask-A-
Nurse, a 24-hour-a-day, seven-days-a-
week free telephone service providing physician referral, community
service referral, and answers to general health questions. Mercy 65 Plus,
a senior membership program, of-

fers discounted health services,
Medicare counseling, and education, as well as a variety of other benefits to its 8,000 members.

In looking toward the 1990s, the
Mercy hospitals plan to maintain
their commitment to the provision
of quality, acute care hospital services. Strategic goals for the 1990s
focus on developing the services at
the local network of hospitals to ensure they continue to reflect the latest advances in medical technology.

Mercy Healthcare Sacramento
looks ahead toward a bright future
in the Sacramento community. As
the population continues to grow,
the hospitals will also grow, adjusting
their services to the community's
needs. Sacramentans and residents
of neighboring communities can
count on the "Mercy Touch" for
generations to come.

UNIVERSITY OF CALIFORNIA, DAVIS

An acknowledged leader in the fields of biological sciences and agriculture, the Davis campus of the University of California is gaining similar recognition for the excellence of its teaching and research in the arts, humanities, social sciences, engineering, health sciences, law, and management.

Under the leadership of Chancellor Theodore L. Hullar, the 85-year-old university opened the new decade with more than 17,000 undergraduates, 3,100 graduate students, and nearly 2,300 professional school students. One of the nation's top 20 universities in research funding, UC Davis has 11 programs rated among the country's top 10, including the number-one botany department.

Founded in 1905, UC Davis is the northernmost of the University of California campuses and occupies 5,200 acres adjacent to the city of Davis, 15 miles west of Sacramento and 72 miles northeast of San Francisco.

From its earliest days as a 778-acre "University Farm" for training in agriculture, UC Davis has grown to offer more than 100 undergraduate and 75 graduate majors in the colleges of Agricultural and Environmental Sciences, Engineering, and Letters and Science. In addition, the university has four professional programs: the School of Law, the Graduate School of Management, the School of Medicine, and the School of Veterinary Medicine, the latter the only such school in California.

The UC Davis Medical Center in Sacramento, the only Class I emergency facility in Northern Califor-

UC Davis students come from every county in California, all 50 states, and about 85 foreign countries.

One of the nation's top 20 research universities, UC Davis remains committed to undergraduate teaching. The university awards an annual $25,000 prize for teaching and scholarly achievement—the largest of its kind in the nation.

nia, operates a regional hospital and trauma center with 470 hospital beds, a regional burn center, a kidney transplant service, and an eye and tissue bank.

UC Davis is one of seven national centers for AIDS research, based on the work under way at the schools of Medicine and Veterinary Medicine and the California Primate Research Center.

The campus has a long history of focused attention on undergraduate education; the arts and languages, history and philosophy, and the sciences are offered as a broad general education combined with specialization in a scholarly discipline. Coupled with this are manifold opportunities for personal development through programs for academic enrichment, internship experiences, and extracurricular student life.

As a university dedicated to research, scholarship, and the education of graduate scholars who will advance the next generations of knowledge, UC Davis offers a highly diverse array of graduate programs, drawing upon the breadth of its specialized academic fields, stimulating cross-disciplinary approaches, and using its distinctive graduate groups.

COLLEGE OF AGRICULTURAL AND ENVIRONMENTAL SCIENCES

In 1905, when the Davis campus was established as a university farm, the foundation was laid for its enduring reputation in agriculture. Today the College of Agricultural and Environmental Sciences includes more than 30 departments, centers, and special institutes devoted to solving technological and

social problems related to food and fiber production and environmental protection. The college is noted for its intellectual range and strength, with many of its programs ranked in the top 10 nationwide, including botany, animal science, genetics, entomology, bacteriology, zoology, and agricultural economics.

COLLEGE OF ENGINEERING

The College of Engineering stresses teaching, research, and public service to solve today's and tomorrow's technological problems in areas such as environmental engineering and water resources; transportation; image processing and computer graphics; geotechnical modeling; lasers and optical-electronics; biochemical and biomedical engineering; computer security; computational fluid dynamics; manufacturing, automation, and productivity; polymeric ultrathin films; and food engineering. The college, established in 1962, has six depart-

Transportation research is but one area of faculty and student interest in the College of Engineering.

ments offering degree programs in chemical engineering; civil and environmental engineering; electrical engineering and computer science; mechanical, aeronautical, and materials engineering; and the only programs in the UC system in applied science and agricultural engineering.

COLLEGE OF LETTERS AND SCIENCE

Established in 1951, Letters and Science is the campus' largest college, with more than 50 departments and programs. It provides instruction and research in such fundamental "liberal arts" disciplines as the humanities, fine arts, social sciences, and natural sciences. Its specialized programs include the Institute of Governmental Affairs, Humanities Institute, Center for Comparative Research, Institute of Theoretical Dynamics, and Crocker

Above: Agricultural and biological sciences at UC Davis are internationally regarded.

Below: Spring cultural festivals celebrate the rich cultural diversity of the campus community.

The preparation of tomorrow's entrepreneurial managers draws together regional business leaders and Graduate School of Management administrators.

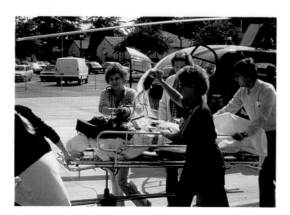

The UC Davis Medical Center's Life Flight helicopter rushes a trauma patient to the center's emergency room. The helicopter averages more than 60 flights per month.

Nuclear Laboratory. The college is distinguished by an exceptionally popular international relations program and renowned programs in several disciplines, including studio art and botany.

SCHOOL OF LAW

With a strongly committed teaching faculty, the School of Law focuses on personalized instruction for its 500 students, through small sections and individualized tutorials. Established in 1965, the school has a highly effective public interest law program and a leading clinical and skills training program, which includes a nationally recognized Immigration Law Clinic. The scholarly productiv-

ity of the senior faculty is highly ranked, and the faculty frequently assists in drafting legislation and multilateral treaties.

GRADUATE SCHOOL OF MANAGEMENT

Established in 1981, the Graduate School of Management grants master's degrees in business administration, engineering management, and management and law. The two-year program emphasizes problem solving and decision making and prepares individuals for high-level management careers in the private and public sectors. The school's fac-

ulty comprises distinguished scholars and professionals of international stature, and its students are among the highest achieving in management programs nationally.

SCHOOL OF MEDICINE/MEDICAL CENTER

The School of Medicine, established in 1966, has 366 faculty members who are conducting more than 325 ongoing research programs in such areas as cardiovascular disease, epidemiology, molecular biology, immunology, clinical nutrition, geriatrics, oncology, eye diseases, and orthopaedic surgery, in addition to a large collaborative effort in the study of AIDS and other retroviral diseases. It is one of the few programs in the nation conducting parallel research on human AIDS and AIDS-like diseases in monkeys, cats, and a variety of other animals. In conjunction with the School of Veterinary Medicine and the California Primate Research Center, the School of Medicine has been designated by the National Institutes of Health as one of seven national centers for AIDS research.

The school's faculty teach and train 372 medical students, 561 interns and residents, 68 family nurse practitioners and physician's assistants, and 70 Ph.D. candidates. Volunteer clinical faculty members, 1,200 in all, support the school's full-time faculty.

The school has made impressive gains in the area of medical student affirmative action: 28 percent of its 1988 entering class were members of underrepresented minorities—the fourth-highest figure among the country's 127 medical schools.

UC Davis Medical Center is the principal teaching and research hospital for the School of Medicine and

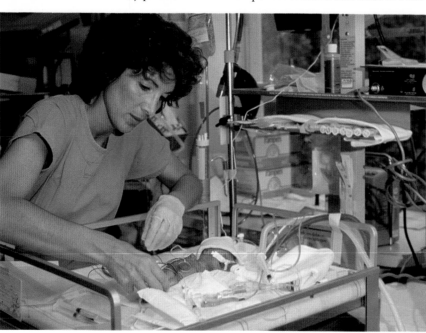

Neonatal intensive care unit nurses and physicians are in attendance around the clock at UC Davis Medical Center.

UC Davis has one of the most successful NCAA Division II athletic programs in the country. Recent national championships were claimed in women's tennis and crew and in men's and women's polo, and the football team holds the NCAA record for consecutive conference titles.

is located on 110 acres in central Sacramento. Through infusion of capital, renovation and construction of facilities, and the arrival of distinguished faculty, the hospital has grown into a leading health sciences campus, devoting its resources to excellence in teaching, research, and patient care.

The UC Davis Medical Center, inland Northern California's only academic medical center, is a 480-bed, fully accredited hospital serving as a major referral center for a 32-county region with a population of more than 4 million residents.

UCDMC and the School of Medicine operate 57 separate facilities on the Sacramento campus. Life Flight, an emergency medical helicopter transport service, averages more than 60 flights per month. UCDMC initiated this program in 1984 to serve critically ill or injured patients from throughout Northern California. The maternal/child transport van, also serving inland Northern California, carries children to both the pediatric and

neonatal intensive care units where nurses and physicians are in attendance around the clock. UCDMC is the only Sacramento-area hospital to have met the rigorous qualifications for membership in the National Association of Children's Hospitals and Related Institutions.

With a 90-95 percent success rate, UCDMC's Department of Ophthalmology provides one of the largest corneal transplant services in the region. The hospital also serves as a vital center for research and treatment of heart disease for both pediatric and adult patients. A new comprehensive cancer treatment center will provide an outpatient service suite, chemotherapy infusion, a conference and patient education center, and ancillary services.

UCD Medical Center's expansion is guided by its newly approved Long Range Development Plan. This ambitious program will help UCDMC meet Northern California's growing health-care needs while maintaining an environment that promotes the pursuit of new knowledge through teaching and research.

With its eight intensive care units, 38-bed trauma nursing unit, more than 100 specialty outpatient medical services, and Regional Poison Control Center, UCDMC is continuing to grow and evolve into a world-class academic medical center.

SCHOOL OF VETERINARY MEDICINE

Established in 1946, the School of Veterinary Medicine is the only veterinary school in the state and is widely regarded as one of the best in the country. It provides outstanding instructional and research programs, including such facilities as the Veterinary Medicine Teaching Hospital, the California Primate Research Center, the California Veterinary Diagnostic Laboratory, the Equine Research Laboratory, and the Veterinary Medical Teaching and Research Center in Tulare. The school has the largest and most diverse research program in the world addressing animal and human health diseases, including programs that range from studies on the molecular level to research concerning whole ecological systems.

The University of California, Davis, is a comprehensive university that is nationally recognized for its teaching and research and highly regarded for its expanding contributions to the Sacramento community.

Top-calibre television directors from London teach and direct theatrical productions on campus through the innovative Granada Artists-in-Residence Program. Internationally prominent speakers and performing arts groups are also frequently featured.

KAISER PERMANENTE

Terese Howard smiled at her four children playing nearby and recalled the weeks of medical care she and the newborns received under the Kaiser Permanente Medical Care Program. All four of her children had been high-risk pregnancies.

"Emotionally and medically the care was the best," said Howard of her seven weeks in maternity and the twins' stay in newborn intensive care.

"When my husband's company changed insurance coverage recently, we stayed with Kaiser. It isn't just the care. It's the caring. It has made me think about becoming a nurse."

More than one in four Northern Californians turn to Kaiser Permanente for their medical care. They are members of the nation's largest private health-care program, serving 6.3 million members from Connecticut to California.

Because Kaiser Permanente runs its own hospitals, laboratories, pharmacies, and medical offices, it provides its members with a complete range of services, from routine physical check-ups, dermatology, and optometry to neurosurgery, newborn intensive care, and genetic counseling. Employers carry the basic coverage and members may pay a fee, which is five dollars or less, whether for a pharmacy prescription or office visit.

"We pride ourselves on being a comprehensive preventive program of affordable health care," says Cliff Skinner, M.D., physician-in-chief, who has been with Kaiser in Sacramento for 25 years.

In the greater Sacramento area, Kaiser Permanente Health Plan members receive medical care from two hospitals and five medical office complexes in the communities of Sacramento, South Sacramento, Roseville, and Davis. As part of a multimillion-dollar local expansion program, within the coming years there will be a hospital in Roseville, a psychiatric hospital in South Sacramento, and a major medical office

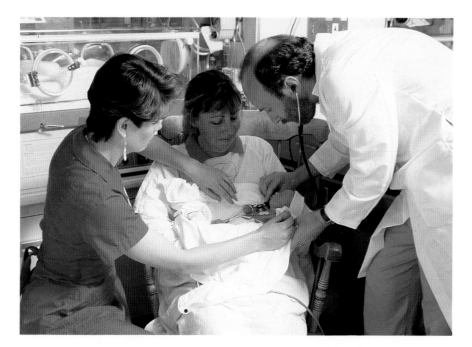

complex in Rancho Cordova.

Members can travel anywhere in the United States and, if a Kaiser Permanente facility is there, receive health care by using their membership card. Kaiser Permanente has facilities in 15 states and the District of Columbia.

Kaiser Permanente physicians, who work in group practice, comprise the largest private medical group in the world. Because office management, equipment purchases, and administration are handled for them, their professional time is given full-time to treating patients, doing research, and expanding skills, rather than running an office, hiring staff, or seeking patients. More than 98 percent of Kaiser Permanente physicians in greater Sacramento are board certified. That means that in addition to completing medical school, residency training, and licensing exams, they have also completed education and training requirements established by national boards of medical specialties.

Kaiser Permanente nurses are among the most extensively educated and trained in the country. In one of the more innovative nursing programs in the state, emphasis is on self-governance, cross-training programs that allow nurses to change

Nearly one-third of the babies born in Sacramento are delivered at Kaiser Permanente.

fields while remaining at the facility, and professional advancements unique to Kaiser Permanente, like the Staff Nurse III recognition given to nurses demonstrating exceptional expertise and outstanding patient involvement.

Kaiser Permanente is a major educational institution in the greater Sacramento area. Serving as the sole affiliated teaching hospital for the University of California, Davis, School of Medicine, Kaiser Permanente provides combined residency programs in all areas, from pediatrics to nuclear medicine. Nearly 50 percent of its physicians are active faculty members at the UC Davis School of Medicine.

Because Kaiser Permanente is committed to preventive health care, the breadth and depth of its health education program is extensive. It provides the largest and most comprehensive community health education program of its type in California. Kaiser Permanente staff teach hundreds of health education classes and programs that are open to the general public. Topics include AIDS, arthritis self-help, living with

Above: As part of its health education program, Kaiser Permanente has three full-time acting troupes that perform at schools in local communities. One of their award-winning productions, the play "Secrets," was described by US News & World Report as "perhaps the most provocative and effective AIDS instruction for teenagers."

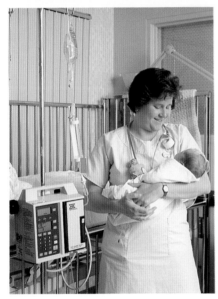

Left: Intensive care for both high-risk pregnancies and newborns is standard coverage at Kaiser Permanente.

cancer, dealing with death, adult diabetes and diet, coping with hearing loss, lowering blood pressure, dealing with anxiety, weight control, smoking cessation, chronic pain management, assertion training, nutrition for teens, women's health, Lamaze training, and parenthood education.

The Emergency Department at Kaiser Permanente is the busiest in the county, handling an average of 60,000 people a year (compared to 35,000 at other medical facilities). The program has pioneered the appropriate use of less costly care like home nursing and the use of nurse practitioners. Kaiser Permanente also delivers more than one

out of every four babies born in Sacramento County, averaging 5,800 babies a year.

Kaiser Permanente is one of the largest hospice providers in the United States. Its programs in Sacramento have won the National Hospice Organization Award of Excellence for three years running. Serving six counties, the hospice program includes hospice-trained volunteers who give home-visit and telephone support.

Approximately 76,000 hours of volunteer services are provided each year by the 455 women, men, and students who donate their time and skills to members, providing everything from delivering flowers and taking pictures of newborns to leading hospital tours and taking blood pressure.

Preventive care is one of the primary concerns of Kaiser Permanente. Members are encouraged to call or come in at the first sign of a

problem. There are more than 30 medical advice nurses whose presence allows members to call and discuss a problem or decide whether or not to seek further care before making an appointment. Personal Health Appraisal is a unique service of Kaiser that educates members in preventive care. Members can sign up for health appraisals at any time and receive extensive education materials. Everyone who joins the Health Plan is encouraged to choose a personal physician.

Founded 45 years ago, Kaiser Permanente was the prototype of the modern health maintenance organization. It evolved from the vision of Sidney Garfield, M.D., who in 1933 established a prepayment medical plan for workers building the Los Angeles aqueduct. In 1938 Edgar Kaiser heard about the successful health-care arrangements on the aqueduct project and persuaded Dr. Garfield to set up a similar plan for the work force building Grand Coulee Dam under Kaiser's management. When the dam was completed, Edgar and his father, Henry J. Kaiser, asked Dr. Garfield to organize group practice prepayment plans for workers at the newly established shipyards they were managing near Oakland and Vancouver. Once World War II ended, Dr. Garfield and the Kaisers decided to make a good plan permanent and opened the program to the community.

"Of all the things I've done, I expect only to be remembered for my hospitals," said Henry J. Kaiser. "They're the things that are filling the people's greatest need—good health."

Successful for the past 45 years, Kaiser Permanente is now seen by some as a model for health plans of the future. Says Alain C. Enthoven, management professor at the Stanford Business School and a well-known specialist in health care, "We as a nation would be much better off if we had a lot more of our care delivered by organized systems like Kaiser."

CALIFORNIA FARM BUREAU FEDERATION

The California Farm Bureau Federation, the voluntary organization made up of most of the family farmers in California, is a proud resident of Sacramento.

Tourists flock to California daily. Its high-technology computer and electronics industries are the finest in the world. Its cities hum with the

During summer months, airline passengers into Sacramento are struck by the hundreds of thousands of acres of shimmering rice fields that produce more than one million tons of rice for consumption in the United States and abroad. The growing, processing, and shipping of rice is a constant economic backbone of

Sacramento's stable economy—just another example of agriculture providing the platform on which an economy is built. The rice storage elevators along the Port of Sacramento and the Sacramento River are evidence of the effect of agriculture on Sacramento.

Rice is not the only crop in Sacramento. In fact, rice is a poor cousin to the tomato in the publicity game. The city is often called the "Big Tomato" or "Sacratomato" by area media and merchants. This moniker is aptly worn since 80 percent of all processing tomatoes in the nation are grown in the region. From late summer well into the fall, thousands of tomato trucks hauling gondolas of the ripe canning variety dot the freeways.

The organization that represents

Left: More than 80 percent of all processing tomatoes in the nation are grown in the region.

Below: A quarter of the jobs in California are in some way related to agriculture.

activity of manufacturing. What is the largest industry in the bustling Golden State? In a state with a population fast approaching 30 million, it comes as a shock to many that the number-one segment of the state economy is agriculture.

The state's number-one industry is the most basic of all—farming. California's farmers produce commodities adding up to a mind-boggling $16 billion at the farm gate, with an effect on the economy reaching more than $50 billion annually. It is one of the state's largest employers; labor experts say that one in four jobs in the state is related in some way to agriculture, from the cultivation of crops to delivery and sale.

The Sacramento region is a hub of agricultural activity, which provides significant energy to the economy of the Capital City area. Rich farmland surrounds the region, providing scenic vistas, economic stimulation, and profitable markets for area businesses.

the farmers who grow rice, tomatoes, and all the 250 diverse commodities produced in California has a long history of service to California and now lists its headquarters in Sacramento.

"We believe Sacramento is the place to be in these challenging, vibrant days," says Bob L. Vice, president of the California Farm Bureau Federation. Vice points out that the private, nonprofit organization moved its headquarters from Berkeley to a 20-acre site in the Point West area near Cal Expo (site of the annual California State Fair) in 1979.

"We studied the length and breadth of the state for the best site for our organization where we could best serve the farmers of the state," explains Vice, a San Diego County avocado grower. "We took more than a year studying our options and then decided unanimously that Sacramento had the economic climate, the quality of life, and the sound political, governmental, and economic stability that we were looking for. In

Right: In 1979 the California Farm Bureau Federation moved its headquarters to a 20-acre site in Sacramento.

Below: The rice storage elevators along the Port of Sacramento are evidence of the effect of agriculture on the region.

the decade that has passed since our move, we have concluded again and again that we made the correct move—no doubt about it."

A recent newspaper study disclosed that the California Farm Bureau Federation, with its more than 85,000 members, is the largest organization headquartered in Sacramento. The Farm Bureau, often mistaken as a government agency because of its name, is unique in many ways. No other organization is formally organized in 56 of the state's 58 counties. Only two counties, Alpine and San Francisco, are not represented by a county Farm Bureau.

Officers of the county and state Farm Bureaus must be bonafide farmers and only members with income from production agriculture may vote in the organization, assur-

ing that the organization will forever be controlled only by those who actually produce the state's food. The organization provides a variety of services to its members, including representation before governmental entities on the national, state, and local levels, as well as information and training activities.

The federation, founded in 1919, is headquartered in Point West, just north of the American River off the Business 80 and State 160 freeways, in a sprawling, top-quality building at the corner of Exposition Boulevard and Heritage Lane, across from the main entrance to Cal Expo. The building won national awards for its innovative energy-conservation system and has been lauded for its architecture and landscaping.

The selection of the building site and the adjacent vacant 16 acres, which is in the planning stage for an upscale office building development, was an easy one, according to Vice.

"Point West gave us the ultimate Sacramento site," says Vice. "The area has strict quality construction restrictions, it is near the geographical center of the metropolitan area, and it is served by excellent transportation systems."

Vice also noted that the Sacramento area's ample supply of quality hotel rooms and meeting facilities provides sites for the many meetings, conventions, and other activities that are an integral part of the activities of the state's largest farm organization.

And, not to be overlooked, the presence of the California Farm Bureau Federation in Sacramento gives the Capital City and its residents a close tie to family farmers throughout the state. Families that provide food and fiber for a growing state and offer stability to an expanding economy.

LINCOLN LAW SCHOOL

Lincoln Law School was created to fill a perceived need for working professionals interested in pursuing a law degree. Today more than 500 graduates attest to the wisdom of the actions taken by Victor A. Bertolani and Andrew J. Smolich in January 1969.

At the time, the two young Sacramento law partners watched with mixed emotions as McGeorge School of Law became accredited by the American Bar Association. Bertolani and Smolich felt McGeorge's pending accreditation would mean higher tuitions, stricter admission policies, and an emphasis on a full-time day program. It was their opinion that this could create a serious problem for Sacramento area students who wanted to attend a high-quality, yet moderately priced, evening law school. They decided to take matters into their own hands. On January 27, 1969, they founded Lincoln University Law School, which was then in charter affiliation with Lincoln University of San Francisco.

The first class of students numbered just 18, but grew to 20 people by the first graduation ceremony in June 1973. Since that memorable June date, more than 500 others have joined the ranks of Lincoln graduates, including such notable professionals as Dave Shore, former Sacramento councilman; Jess Bedore III, chief deputy of the Placer County District Attorney's Office; Doug Nareau, Eureka district attorney; and Bruce Nestande, a member of the Orange County Board of Supervisors.

Currently, more than 200 working professionals attend classes at the second-floor midtown campus. Lincoln Law School is administered by cofounder Andrew Smolich, who serves as executive dean and is a member of the school's Academic Advisory Board, and his wife, Marilyn, who serves as business manager. The husband/wife duo became the sole proprietors of the school in 1985.

Academic support is provided by

Charles D'Arcy III, academic dean; Dean S.L. Roullier, administrative dean; Jeannie Kunz, registrar; and Patricia Latteri, librarian. Lincoln Law School also employs as faculty members of the Sacramento County court system. According to executive Dean Smolich, these trial lawyers and judges bring practical, up-to-date instruction to law-school classrooms, keeping students abreast of the constantly changing legal profession.

The four-year Lincoln Law School program is divided into two 18-week semesters per year, with a six-week summer session. Fall and spring semesters meet three nights a week; the summer session meets four evenings a week. A minimum of 86 units is required for graduation.

Located at 3140 J Street in Sacramento, Lincoln Law School is just minutes from the California State Capitol, the U.S. District Court, California's Third District Court of Appeals, the Sacramento County Law Library, the California State Law Library, and the superior and municipal courts. Situated off Business 80, the school is easily accessible from all Sacramento freeways.

Practical experience at the student level is stressed at Lincoln Law School. Required courses are used as a foundation for understanding the law, with elective and experiential opportunities designed to broaden and diversify the student's background.

Throughout its 20 years, Lincoln Law School has maintained a policy of considering the total person when screening applicants. Transfer students are welcomed and students who may not have succeeded in another law school will often be given the extra attention needed to make the most of a second chance.

Left: Since 1973 more than 500 Sacramento professionals have graduated from Lincoln Law School.

Below: More than 200 working professionals currently attend classes at Lincoln Law School's midtown campus.

HEALD BUSINESS COLLEGE

For more than 125 years Heald Business Colleges have been preparing students throughout California for the job market. In Sacramento, at the new Rancho Cordova campus, Heald Business College and the new Heald Institute of Technology annually train hundreds of students through day and evening programs that provide them with the skills needed to get a job in today's marketplace.

"Heald programs emphasize computer skills because that's where business and technology are going," explains David B. Raulston, vice president and director of the Sacramento campus. "We provide students with a state-of-the-art career education. Our placement people take it from there."

Heald placement specialists offer job counseling and interview training. According to Raulston, 95 percent of Heald College graduates from Sacramento are placed in jobs within three months of graduation.

"After graduation, Heald arranges job interviews for students until we find the job the student wants," says Raulston. "Heald's placement service is available to students forever."

Heald Business College, which is located near Sunrise and Highway 50 in Rancho Cordova, teaches students the knowledge and skills which will earn them the most promising jobs available in business and industry.

Heald Business College is accredited by the Accrediting Commission for Community and Junior Colleges of the Western Association of Schools and Colleges. It is one of the few two-year business education institutions to have such an accreditation in California.

The purpose of Heald Business College is to prepare students with the knowledge and skills that will enable them to qualify for entry-level jobs in business and industry in the shortest possible period of time. Emphasis is placed on practical job-oriented instruction. Training is designed to develop analytical problem-solving skills, mature levels of

conduct, and the attitudes, values, and habits required for career advancement.

This commitment to "Excellence in Education" began in 1863, when Edward Payson Heald rented a room in San Francisco to use as a classroom for teaching business subjects to three students. During the 1860s the Heald curriculum was limited to bookkeeping, penmanship, arithmetic, and law. During the 1870s and 1880s the typewriter, telephone, and adding machine were invented, and the curriculum was expanded to accommodate these new business office innovations.

Throughout the next 100 years, Heald curriculum has stayed abreast with employment trends and technology developments. The college also grew right along with the state, adding campuses as new metropolitan regions developed. The first Sacramento campus opened downtown in 1908.

Today Heald Colleges is comprised of five Heald Institute of Technology campuses and 10 Heald Business College campuses located throughout California. In 1978 Heald Colleges was chartered by the State of California as a nonprofit educational system and approved by the federal government as a tax exempt nonprofit corporation.

MARSHALL HOSPITAL

Since 1957, when a small group of concerned citizens in the Placerville area formed the Marshall Hospital Corporation, Marshall Hospital has been a community health facility of the people, by the people, and for the people.

Named after James Marshall, who discovered gold at Sutter's Mill a few miles away from the hospital site, the facility was established as a nonprofit community hospital that would have a local board of directors to represent the needs and interests of a growing El Dorado community.

On July 1, 1959, a dedicated handful of employees first opened the doors to the new 50-bed hospital. The first maternity patient that day gave birth to twin boys. The community and its hospital has been growing ever since. Today there are approximately 165 doctors affiliated with Marshall Hospital. They work closely with the administration and board of directors in both policy and operational issues.

As Marshall Hospital entered the 1990s, the first $4-million phase of the 7.4-acre Marshall Hospital Professional Center was opened to the public. Phase I of the development of the hospital's new medical and health services campus includes approximately 28,000 square feet spread among five buildings. The hospital purchased these 7.4 acres in the Goldorado Center development in 1987 and retains an option on an adjacent 10-acre parcel.

The new professional center opened with 17 different physician specialties represented. The core building on the campus already houses clinical laboratory and diagnostic imaging services, as well as a conference center. A variety of classes for both health professionals and the general public are conducted on this convenient site. Furthermore, this is the location of

Above: The CT scanner plays a critical diagnostic role for the very busy emergency services department. Located just off Highway 50 between Sacramento and South Lake Tahoe, the hospital takes care of many injuries associated with all the year-round recreational activities in the forest service and wilderness areas.

Below: To better serve El Dorado County, a new 7.4-acre medical campus was opened in Cameron Park in 1990. The first phase includes five buildings which house physician office suites representing 16 specialties, as well as a physical therapy and work hardening center, diagnostic imaging facilities, a clinical lab, and a conference center.

the local magnetic resonance imaging (MRI) service.

Future construction phases or addition of services could easily encompass anything from a surgicenter, or a minor emergency clinic, to new diagnostic services and physician suites.

Future construction phases or addition of services within the initial set of buildings are primarily dependent on the actual demand for specific services as the community grows.

"Marshall Hospital is also continuing to expand and improve services at its main site in Placerville," notes Juli Miller, public relations director for the hospital. "We are constantly evaluating what services should be offered, where, and in what way in order to keep medical care economical, safe, and convenient for our community."

Due to a dramatic increase in the number of surgeries performed at the main hospital during the latter part of the 1980s, an $11-million surgery center was added in 1989. The new center features a separate outpatient surgery department. Much like a freestanding surgicenter, it has its own entrance, lobbies, patient preparation and recovery areas, and nursing staff. This is where procedures such as arthoscopies, cataract removals, endoscopies, and tonsillectomies are performed. The emphasis continues to be in reducing the amount of time spent in a hospital, not only because it reduces costs, but it also returns the patient to the best healing environment—the home.

An additional $6 million was spent on capital-equipment purchases during the late 1980s. The facility's medical capabilities were enhanced by the purchase of new cardiac monitoring systems, surgical anesthesia equipment, mammography, and imaging machines. Miller notes this is considered a large capital improvement for a small community hospital.

Today's Marshall Hospital is a 90-bed fully accredited acute care hospital. It features a base-station emergency department for the emergency medic units dispatched throughout the Western Slope of El Dorado County. The hospital's entire staff of physicians schedule themselves to support the hospital emergency department with the necessary spectrum of medical/surgical specialties around the clock. It has an eight-bed intensive care/cardiac care unit, a maternity/nursery unit, two medical/surgical floors, and several off-site lab and X-ray stations for the convenience of patients.

The hospital and the new professional center feature several programs designed to service the needs of the community. The hospital has long offered cardiac rehabilitation/ pulmonary rehabilitation programs, while the new center now offers the Physical Edge and Fit to Work programs.

The Physical Edge is a physical therapy, assessment, and training program. In addition to providing routine physical therapy, it emphasizes sports medicine and returning an athlete to a specific athletic activity as soon as possible or preparing someone to begin participation in a specific sport. Its staff includes physical therapists, exercise physiologists, and athletic trainers.

Fit to Work serves those who have been injured at work. Its staff includes physical therapists and occu-

Marshall Mouse is the beloved mascot for the children at the hospital, and he makes guest appearances at various events in the community. About 200 enthusiastic volunteers, dressed in pink, also lend a special touch to this medical center, doing everything from operating the gift shop to assisting with patients and families in the emergency department.

pational therapists who assist the physician in evaluating the physical work capacity of employees after an injury. A customized "work hardening" program can then be developed and supervised to prepare the employee to return to work with

maximum strength, endurance, functional abilities, knowledge of worker safety guidelines, and a confidence in his or her ability to return to the workplace.

Although it has come a long way since that 50-bed facility first opened in 1959, Marshall Hospital continues to have very strong links with the community. Its board of directors is comprised of 11 community volunteers who each serve three-year terms. The Marshall Hospital Auxiliary is made up of almost 200 patrons, volunteers, and junior volunteers who provide services to patients, visitors, and hospital staff daily. Popular annual fund-raising activities include the annual Pink Lady's Marketplace, the Walk-a-thon, and the Christmas Bake Sale. The volunteers also operate the popular hospital gift shop.

The facility also boasts a close affiliation with the Marshall Hospital Foundation, which has a goal to support the long-term financial stability of the hospital through an endowment fund, several annual fund-raising events, and other planned giving programs. The Citizens Advisory Committee, which has representatives from community special-interest groups and service organizations, meets monthly with the hospital administrator.

The new outpatient surgery center opened in the fall of 1989. It is in this new complex that those patients who have cataract surgery, arthroscopies, ear tube insertions, laser and endoscopic procedures, and cosmetic surgery are cared for in private, sun-filled rooms during their few hours at the center.

ESKATON

If one idea or goal has remained unchanged throughout Eskaton's 23-year history, it is the high quality of life for patients and residents. That is the commitment made in Oakland in 1967, when Eskaton became a health-care organization. Today, from beginnings of just one facility to 40-plus, Eskaton remains steadfast in its approach to keeping quality of life in every aspect of its operation.

That goal has directed Eskaton for more than two decades, and it has continually been applied to a variety of innovative, yet complementary, areas of service. From acute care hospitals, to home delivery of meals, to retirement communities, to nursing facilities throughout Northern California, Eskaton has led the

way in meeting the needs of all segments of the population. Today, the focus of Eskaton points towards care and services for the retired and elderly, a dramatic shift from early days when acute care hospitals were Eskaton's mainstay.

Beginning in 1968 with the purchase of the 250-bed American River Hospital in Carmichael, Eskaton started the reputation it enjoys today. Eskaton soon bought Mount Shasta Community Hospital, Colusa Community Hospital, and the Community Hospital of Monterey. At about the same time that Eskaton was serving these and other rural communities, evaluation began on a cluster-of-care concept aimed at providing a spectrum of services in a va-

This artist's rendering of Eskaton Village's 37 acres located on Walnut Avenue in Carmichael reveals a community designed for active living. A gated entrance with a lake just beyond provides a dramatic prelude to The Village Center—the focal point of the community which boasts everything from a resident's business center to an elegant restaurant-style dining room.

riety of facilities, with a cost savings for the user. With this plan as a guide, Eskaton began providing services for the elderly population, and soon started building retirement communities and other facilities that offered both independent living and other types of care and programs.

The first major project began in 1973 with the construction of President James Monroe Manor in

Sacramento's south area. This 120-unit high-rise independent living facility stands out as one of the area's success stories in retirement living. Two years later, Eskaton followed with Annadale Manor—Sacramento's first sizable residential care facility.

A formal commitment to services for the elderly and retired was now underway. A succession of firsts followed rapidly. In 1978 Eskaton opened its first skilled nursing facility, Eskaton Manzanita Manor. In 1979 President Thomas Jefferson Manor, Eskaton's initial rent-subsidized senior housing facility, began accepting applications.

Eskaton moved quickly to meet the growing needs of older citizens in Northern California. The impact on life in Sacramento and other communities was becoming very evident, and Eskaton's unique ability to offer personal attention to patients and residents was making a difference in many lives.

While progress continued with the construction and purchase of facilities throughout Northern California, Eskaton took the next logical step in its cluster-of-care concept—home health. Through a merger with the Sacramento Visiting Nurse Association (VNA), Eskaton began providing in-home health care in 1981. Today, as part of Eskaton's support services division, VNA annually makes more than 100,000 home visits. As an adjunct to all of the Eskaton programs, Meals for Friends, a below-cost home delivery service, was also started about the same time.

Eskaton continued to grow into the 1980s. A 128-bed intermediate care facility, Eskaton Glenwood Manor, was acquired; the Yolo Adult Day Health Care Center was built in Woodland; and Eskaton's first psychiatric skilled nursing facility, Eskaton American River Manor, was purchased.

Responding to need and economic trends, the Eskaton board decided in 1986 to concentrate exclusively on the care of the retired and elderly. The stand-alone hospi-

Eskaton president John Breaux points out a feature of Eskaton Village, in Carmichael, which is a planned 37-acre lifecare retirement community.

tal in Northern California was becoming increasingly competitive—an industry shakeout loomed on the horizon. A partner for Eskaton American River Hospital and Eskaton's long-term care operations was sought, and an agreement with the Alta Bates Corp. of Berkeley was reached.

Subsequently, Eskaton chief executive officer John Breaux unveiled plans for "the first life-care housing community in the Sacramento area." Eskaton Village is a $60-million complex to be located in Carmichael and designed to provide lifetime care and living accommodations for the independent senior.

What distinguishes a life-care facility from other forms of retirement housing is the multiple levels of care provided and the payment of a membership fee for the right to live in the community. Also, up to 90 percent of the purchase price and 50 percent of

any appreciation can be realized on the resale of a membership.

The 260 apartments and 84 cottages, along with 40 assisted-living units, will be built around a 48,000-square-foot community center, which will contain meeting rooms, lounges, a dance floor, library, hair care and craft shops, guest accommodations, and staff offices. In addition, the site at Walnut Avenue and Gibbons Drive also will have a pool, spa, barbecue, and picnic areas.

"The village will combine Eskaton's years of retirement and nursing care experience into one 37-acre campuslike setting that will offer residents a comprehensive and secure approach to both retirement and long-term care," says Breaux.

Patrons

The following individuals, companies, and organizations have made a valuable commitment to the quality of this publication. Windsor Publications gratefully acknowledges their participation in *Sacramento: Heart of California*.

American Airlines*
California Farm Bureau Federation*
Capital Power Federal Credit Union*
C.C. Myers, Inc.*
Commerce Security Bank*
Dokken Engineering*
Eskaton*
Frank Fat, Inc.*
Greve, Clifford, Diepenbrock & Paras*
GTEL*

Harding Lawson Associates*
Heald Business College*
Hyatt Regency Sacramento at Capitol Park*
Kaiser Permanente*
KFBK/Y92*
Kronick, Moskovitz, Tiedemann & Girard*
Leason Pomeroy Associates, Inc.*
Lincoln Law School*
Maloney and Bell, General Contractors, Inc.*
Marshall Hospital*
MCI Communications Corporation*
McLaren/Hart Environmental Engineering Corporation*
Mercy Healthcare Sacramento*
M.J. Brock & Sons, Inc.*
Pacific Gas & Electric*

Red Lion Hotels & Inns*
Robert E. Young Engineers*
Sunrise Bank of California*
Tenco*
3DI, Inc.*
Town & Country*
University of California, Davis*
Wells Fargo Bank*
William Glen*
Wraith & Associates, Inc.*

*Participants in Part Two, "Sacramento's Enterprises." The stories of these companies and organizations appear in chapters 7 through 12, beginning on page 105.

Photo by Bob Rowan/Progressive Image Photography

Directory of Corporate Sponsors

American Airlines, pp. 106-107
1750 Home Avenue, #510
Sacramento, CA 95825
916/924-1404
Lee C. Reichert

California Farm Bureau Federation,
176-177
1601 Exposition Boulevard
Sacramento, CA 95815
916/924-4075
George J. Gomes

Capital Power Federal Credit Union,
146
6341 Folsom Boulevard
Sacramento, CA 95819
916/452-4215
Mary McPoil

C.C. Myers, Inc., 152-153
3286 Fitzgerald
Rancho Cordova, CA 95742
916/635-9370
C.C. Myers

Commerce Security Bank, 144-145
1545 River Park Drive
Sacramento, CA 95815
916/922-9500
G.G. Michel

Dokken Engineering, 160
3221 Ramos Circle
Sacramento, CA 95827
916/361-3111
Richard A. Dokken

Eskaton, 182-183
5105 Manzanita Avenue
Carmichael, CA 95608
916/334-0810
Jerry P. Jones

Frank Fat, Inc., 133
1015 Front Street
Sacramento, CA 95814
916/441-4184
Jerry Fat

Greve, Clifford, Diepenbrock &
Paras, 118-119
1000 G Street, Suite 400
Sacramento, CA 95814
916/443-2011
Lawrence Wengel

GTEL, 110-111
One GTE Place
Thousand Oaks, CA 91362
805/372-7884
B.B. Heiler

Harding Lawson Associates, 161
10324 Placer Lane
Sacramento, CA 95827
916/364-0793
Ambrose McCready

Heald Business College, 179
2910 Prospect Park Drive
Rancho Cordova, CA 95670
916/638-1616
David B. Raulston

Hyatt Regency Sacramento at
Capitol Park, 128-131
1209 L Street
Sacramento, CA 95814
916/443-1234
David Shultz

Kaiser Permanente, 174-175
2025 Morse Avenue
Sacramento, CA 95825-2115
916/973-7930
Mary Jo Rogers

KFBK/Y92, 108-109
1440 Ethan Way, #200
Sacramento, CA 95825
916/926-5325
Joyce Krieg

Kronick, Moskovitz, Tiedemann &
Girard, 120-121
770 L Street, Suite 1200
Sacramento, CA 95814
916/444-8920
Rosmarie F. Skinner

Leason Pomeroy Associates, Inc.,
154
1215 G Street
Sacramento, CA 95814
916/443-0335
John Gack

Lincoln Law School, 178
3140 J Street
Sacramento, CA 95816
916/446-1275
Marilyn Smolich

Maloney and Bell, General
Contractors, Inc., 150-151
2718 Mercantile Drive
Rancho Cordova, CA 95742
916/635-7600
Robert A. Bell

Marshall Hospital, 180-181
Marshall Way
Placerville, CA 95667
916/626-2645
Juli Miller

MCI Communications Corporation,
114
201 Spear Street
San Francisco, CA 94105
415/978-1450
Michelle Payer

McLaren/Hart Environmental
Engineering Corporation, 162-163
11101 White Rock Road
Rancho Cordova, CA 95670
916/638-3696
Mary Lynn Hollingsworth

Mercy Healthcare Sacramento,
168-169
2710 Gateway Oaks Drive, Suite 300N
Sacramento, CA 95833
916/648-3700
Cynthia A. Holst

M.J. Brock & Sons, Inc., 156-159
3350 Watt Avenue
Sacramento, CA 95821
916/488-4500
Donald E. Reed

Photo by Bob Rowan/Progressive Image
Photography

Pacific Gas & Electric, 112-113
2740 Gateway Oaks
Sacramento, CA 95833
916/923-7017
Stephen P. Gale

Red Lion Hotels & Inns, 132
2001 Point West Way
Sacramento, CA 95815
916/929-8855
Kelley Johnson

Robert E. Young Engineers, 155
3222 Ramos Circle
Sacramento, CA 95827
916/366-3040
Robert E. Young

Sunrise Bank of California, 138-139
5 Sierra Tate Plaza
Roseville, CA 95678
916/786-7080
Jeanie Hagen-Greene

Tenco, 134-135
7310 Pacific Avenue
Pleasant Grove, CA 95668
916/991-8223
J.R. Brooks

3DI, Inc., 164
501 J Street, Suite 200
Sacramento, CA 95814
916/447-7600
Terrie Becker

Town & Country, 127
1620 McClaren Drive
Carmichael, CA 95608
Marcy Friedman

University of California, Davis,
170-173
Davis, CA 95616
916/752-2067
Larry Vanderhalf

Wells Fargo Bank, 140-143
One Packdenter Drive
Sacramento, CA 95825
916/440-4017
Margaret L. Kane

William Glen, 126
2651 El Paseo Lane
Sacramento, CA 95821
916/485-3000
William C. Snyder

Wraith & Associates, Inc., 122
1745 Markston Road, Suite 200
Sacramento, CA 95825
916/920-8500
Ron Blickle

Bibliography

Chapter 1

Federal Writers' Project. *The WPA Guide to California.* New York: Pantheon Books, 1939.

Gunsky, Fred, and Mary Griffith, eds. *Sacramento Yesterday.* From *Golden Notes Quarterly.* Sacramento: Sacramento Historical Society, 1988.

Leland, Dorothea Kupcha. *A Short History of Sacramento.* San Francisco: Lexicos Books, 1989.

Smith, Day, Wilcox, et. al. *Sketches of Old Sacramento.* Sacramento: Sacramento County Historical Society, 1976.

Wyman, Walker D., ed. *California Emigrant Letters.* New York: AMS Press, 1971. (Reprint of 1952 edition.)

Zollinger, James Peter. *Sutter: The Man And His Empire.* London: Oxford University Press, 1939.

Chapter 2

Davis, Win. J. *An Illustrated History of Sacramento County.* Chicago: The Lewis Publishing Company, 1890.

Downtown Sacramento Redevelopment Plan Update. John M. Sanger Associates Inc. July 1983.

Horowitz, Bob. "Begging to Build: Four Developers Court City for Lot A." *Sacramento News & Review* October 19, 1989.

Sacramento Housing & Redevelopment Agency and Sacramento Department of City Planning. *Sacramento Urban Design Plan.* 3 vols. 1987.

Severson, Thor. *Sacramento: An Illustrated History, 1839-1874, From Sutter's Fort to Capitol City.* California Historical Society, 1973.

Chapter 3

Burness, Robert C., and J. Richard Blackmarr. *The Sacramento Region in 1990, Economic Growth and the Demand for Industrial Land.* Sacramento: Sacramento County Planning and Community Development Department, 1982.

California State University Sacramento Real Estate and Land Use Institute. *Business Profile.* Sacramento: Sacramento Area Commerce and Trade Organization, Winter 1989.

McGowan, Joseph A. *A History of the Sacramento Valley.* New York and Palm Beach: Lewis Publishing Company, 1961.

Miller, Maurice A., ed. *McClellan Air Force Base 1936-1982, A Pictorial History.* Sacramento: Office of History, Sacramento Air Logistics Center, 1982.

"Sacramento 150, A Sesquicentennial Celebration 1839-1989." 3-part series. *Sacramento Bee* July 30, 1989.

Chapter 4

Craft, George S., et al. *CSUS: The First Forty Years: 1947-1987.* Hornet Foundation, 1987.

Shields, Peter J. *The Birth of an Institution: The Agricultural College at Davis.* Sacramento: Self-published, 1954.

Willis, William L. *History of Sacramento County, California.* Los Angeles: Historic Record Company, 1913.

Sacramento Bee. Articles on early hospitals: September 19, 1922; February 16, 1965; May 17, 1970.

Sacramento Union. Articles on Sacramento County Hospital: March 13 & 19, 1868.

Chapter 5

Berthelsen, Gene, ed. *Sacramento Dixieland Jubilee: 10th Annual Guidebook.* Sacramento: Dailey, Berthelsen & Associates, 1983.

Glackin, William. "Music & Dance in Spades." *Sacramento Bee* July 30, 1989.

Haugen, Peter. "For Theatergoers, Curtain Rises on a New Era." *Sacramento Bee* July 29, 1990.

Kurutz, Ed. "Sacramento's Pioneer Patrons of Art." *Golden Notes* 31:2 Summer 1985.

Leland, Dorothea Kupcha. *A Short History of Sacramento.* San Francisco: Lexicos Books, 1989.

Chapter 6

Coe, Karen. "The Parkway." *Sacramento Magazine* August 1989.

Fie, Julie, and Bill Stevens. *Media Guide Yearbook, 1989-1990.* Sacramento: Sacramento Kings, 1989.

Gardner, Earle Stanley. *Drifting Down the Delta.* New York: William Morrow & Co., 1969.

MacCormack, Frank Xavier. *Never Lose: A Decade of Sports and Politics in Sacramento.* Rancho Cordova, Calif.: First Ink, 1989.

Index

Photo by Mark E. Gibson

Photo Identification
The Fine Arts Museum of San
    Francisco, gift of M.H. de Young
    Endowment Fund: Pages 10-11:
Sacramento Railroad Station by
    William Hahn, 1874, oil on
    canvas mounted board
    53 3/4" x 87 3/4" -